Clear**Revise**™

Edexcel GCSE
Computer Science 1CP2

Illustrated revision and practice

Published by
PG Online Limited
The Old Coach House
35 Main Road
Tolpuddle
Dorset
DT2 7EW
United Kingdom

sales@pgonline.co.uk
www.pgonline.co.uk
2020

PG ONLINE

PREFACE

Absolute clarity! That's the aim.

This is everything you need to ace your exam and beam with pride. Each topic is laid out in a beautifully illustrated format that is clear, approachable and as concise and simple as possible.

Each section of the specification is clearly indicated to help you cross-reference your revision. The checklist on the contents pages will help you keep track of what you have already worked through and what's left before the big day.

We have included worked examination-style questions with answers for almost every topic. This helps you understand where marks are coming from and to see the theory at work for yourself in an examination situation. There is also a set of exam-style questions at the end of each section for you to practise writing answers for. You can check your answers against those given at the end of the book.

LEVELS OF LEARNING

Based on the degree to which you are able to truly understand a new topic, we recommend that you work in stages. Start by reading a short explanation of something, then try and recall what you've just read. This has limited effect if you stop there but it aids the next stage. Question everything. Write down your own summary and then complete and mark a related exam-style question. Cover up the answers if necessary but learn from them once you've seen them. Lastly, teach someone else. Explain the topic in a way that they can understand. Have a go at the different practice questions – they offer an insight into how and where marks are awarded.

ACKNOWLEDGEMENTS

The questions in the ClearRevise textbook are the sole responsibility of the authors and have neither been provided nor approved by the examination board.

Every effort has been made to trace and acknowledge ownership of copyright. The publishers will be happy to make any future amendments with copyright owners that it has not been possible to contact. The publisher would like to thank the following companies and individuals who granted permission for the use of their images or material in this textbook.

Examination structure: © Pearson Education Ltd

Design and artwork: Jessica Webb / PG Online Ltd
Graphics / images: © Shutterstock

First edition 2020. 10 9 8 7 6 5 4 3 2
A catalogue entry for this book is available from the British Library
ISBN: 978-1-910523-28-5
Copyright © PG Online 2020

Printed on FSC certified paper by Bell and Bain Ltd, Glasgow, UK.

THE SCIENCE OF REVISION

Illustrations and words

Research has shown that revising with words and pictures doubles the quality of responses by students.[1] This is known as 'dual-coding' because it provides two ways of fetching the information from our brain. The improvement in responses is particularly apparent in students when asked to apply their knowledge to different problems. Recall, application and judgement are all specifically and carefully assessed in public examination questions.

Retrieval of information

Retrieval practice encourages students to come up with answers to questions.[2] The closer the question is to one you might see in a real examination, the better. Also, the closer the environment in which a student revises is to the 'examination environment', the better. Students who had a test 2-7 days away did 30% better using retrieval practice than students who simply read, or repeatedly reread material. Students who were expected to teach the content to someone else after their revision period did better still.[3] What was found to be most interesting in other studies is that students using retrieval methods and testing for revision were also more resilient to the introduction of stress.[4]

Ebbinghaus' forgetting curve and spaced learning

Ebbinghaus' 140-year-old study examined the rate in which we forget things over time. The findings still hold power. However, the act of forgetting things and relearning them is what cements things into the brain.[5] Spacing out revision is more effective than cramming – we know that, but students should also know that the space between revisiting material should vary depending on how far away the examination is. A cyclical approach is required. An examination 12 months away necessitates revisiting covered material about once a month. A test in 30 days should have topics revisited every 3 days – intervals of roughly a tenth of the time available.[6]

Summary

Students: the more tests and past questions you do, in an environment as close to examination conditions as possible, the better you are likely to perform on the day. If you prefer to listen to music while you revise, tunes without lyrics will be far less detrimental to your memory and retention. Silence is most effective.[5] If you choose to study with friends, choose carefully – effort is contagious.[7]

1.   Mayer, R. E., & Anderson, R. B. (1991). Animations need narrations: An experimental test of dual-coding hypothesis. *Journal of Education Psychology*, (83)4, 484–490.

2.   Roediger III, H. L., & Karpicke, J.D. (2006). Test-enhanced learning: Taking memory tests improves long-term retention. *Psychological Science*, 17(3), 249–255.

3.   Nestojko, J., Bui, D., Kornell, N. & Bjork, E. (2014). Expecting to teach enhances learning and organisation of knowledge in free recall of text passages. *Memory and Cognition*, 42(7), 1038–1048.

4.   Smith, A. M., Floerke, V. A., & Thomas, A. K. (2016) Retrieval practice protects memory against acute stress. *Science*, 354(6315), 1046–1048.

5.   Perham, N., & Currie, H. (2014). Does listening to preferred music improve comprehension performance? *Applied Cognitive Psychology*, 28(2), 279–284.

6.   Cepeda, N. J., Vul, E., Rohrer, D., Wixted, J. T. & Pashler, H. (2008). Spacing effects in learning a temporal ridgeline of optimal retention. *Psychological Science*, 19(11), 1095–1102.

7.   Busch, B. & Watson, E. (2019), *The Science of Learning*, 1st ed. Routledge.

CONTENTS

Paper 1   Principles of Computer Science

Topic 1   Computational thinking   ☑

Specification

Topic 2   Data   ☑

Topic 3   Computers

☑

Topic 4   Networks

☑

Topic 5   Issues and impact

☑

MARK ALLOCATIONS

Green mark allocations[1] on answers to in-text questions through this guide help to indicate where marks are gained within the answers. A bracketed '1' e.g. [1] = one valid point worthy of a mark. There are often many more points to make than there are marks available so you have more opportunity to max out your answers than you may think.

TOPICS FOR PAPER 1
PRINCIPLES OF COMPUTER SCIENCE
(1CP2/01)

Information about Paper 1

Written exam: 1 hour and 30 minutes
75 marks
50% of GCSE

Specification coverage

Computational thinking, data, computers, networks, and issues and impact.

The content for this assessment will be drawn from Topics 1 to 5 of the specification.

Questions

This paper consists of five compulsory questions, each one focused on one of the major topic areas. The questions will use multiple-choice, short answer and extended response styles. Tables and diagrams will also be used.

DECOMPOSITION AND ABSTRACTION

Computational thinking

Computational thinking is a process used to solve complex problems. It means formulating a problem and expressing its solution in such a way that a computer can carry it out.

There are two important stages involved:

- **Abstraction** involves identifying the key parts of the problem and removing any unnecessary detail so that it becomes easier to solve. For example, if a program is to be written to simulate a card game, the first task to be accomplished may be 'shuffle the cards'. This is an abstraction – implementing it will involve specifying a way to randomise the order of 52 values representing the cards. We can refer to 'shuffle' throughout the program without specifying how it will be done.

- **Decomposition** means breaking down a complex problem into smaller, manageable parts which are easier to solve. This comprises the following steps:
  - o Identify the main problem
  - o List the main sub-problems, functions or tasks
  - o Break these down into smaller **sub-problems** or sub-tasks which can then be completed separately.

A self-driving car is being developed. The software has to be capable of distinguishing between an animal and a person crossing the road in front of the car.

(a) Define what is meant by **abstraction**. [2]

(b) Give **one** example of how abstraction could be used in developing this software. [1]

(a) Removing / hiding details of a problem[1] that are not relevant to a solution[1].

(b) Any example of something that can be removed or hidden, e.g. speed of the car[1], location at which something is crossing[1], whether it is on a pedestrian crossing[1], aerodynamic design of the vehicle[1].

Benefits of using subprograms

Decomposition of a problem involves breaking down a problem into subroutines or **modules**.

Using subroutines in programs has many advantages

- Makes debugging and maintaining the program easier as subroutines are usually no more than a page of code and are separate from the main program
- Subroutines can be tested separately and shown to be correct
- A particular subroutine can be called several times in the same program, and may also be saved in a subroutine library to be used in other programs

USING FLOWCHARTS

Flowcharts are a useful tool that can be used to develop solutions to a problem. Standard flowchart symbols are shown below:

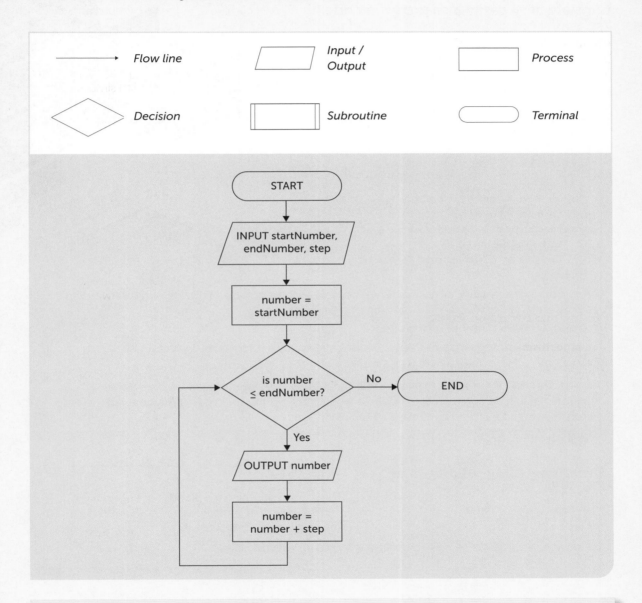

Look at the flowchart above.

(a) What will be output if the user enters 7, 50, 10 for the three input values? [2]

(b) What will be output if the user enters an end number which is less than the start number? [1]

(a) 7[1], 17, 27, 37, 47[1]

(b) Nothing will be output.[1]

PSEUDOCODE AND ALGORITHMS

The problem with using a flowchart to develop an algorithm is that it does not usually translate very easily into program code.

Pseudocode is useful for developing an algorithm using programming-style constructs, but it is not an actual programming language. This means that a programmer can concentrate on figuring out how to solve the problem without worrying about the details of how to write each statement in the programming language that will be used.

Using pseudocode, the algorithm shown in the flowchart on page 3 could be expressed like this:

```
input startNumber, endNumber, step
set number to startNumber
while number <= endNumber
    output(number)
    add step to number
endwhile
```

Follow and write algorithms

An **algorithm** is a sequence of steps that can be followed in order to complete a task. Examples include recipes, assembly instructions and directions.

An algorithm is not the same as a computer program. A computer program is one way of implementing an algorithm in a particular language, but it is the series of instructions and the order of those instructions that are the basis of any algorithm.

In this paper, you may be given a flowchart and asked to determine the purpose of the algorithm.

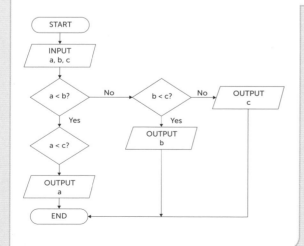

Determine the purpose of the algorithm shown in the flowchart. [1]

The purpose is to output the smallest of three values.[1]

This algorithm uses a **nested selection** structure.

The IF statement (or decision) has an IF statement nested inside it. In this example, the ELSE statement also has a nested IF statement.

FOLLOWING AND WRITING ALGORITHMS

Instead of using a flowchart, you could write the algorithm on the opposite page in pseudocode:

```
input a, b, c
if a < b
    if a < c
        print "Smallest value is" a
else
    if b < c
        print "Smallest value is" b
    else
        print "Smallest value is" c
```

> Try following through the algorithm with test data a = 5, b = 3, c = 6. Try two more sets of test data, a = 1, b = 3, c = 6 and a = 5, b = 3, c = 2. Does the algorithm always give the correct result?

Which do you find easier to follow, the flowchart or the pseudocode? Notice how important the indentation is in the pseudocode. It indicates which "else" belongs to each "if".

In Section 6.3, you will learn to write and follow algorithms that involve one- and two-dimensional lists, arithmetic, relational and logical operators.

Algorithms which involve sorting data held in a one-dimensional list, or searching for an item in a list, are covered in Section 1.2.6.

Arrays and lists

Arrays are not generally used in Python. The equivalent data structure is a **list**, which is a collection of variables of the same or different types, enclosed in square brackets.

```
playerName = ["Corrie", "Ben", "Gordon", "Lennie", "Pete"]
```

Each item in a list is referenced using an **index**, starting at 0 for the first item.

`first = playerName[0]` will assign `"Corrie"` to the variable `first`.

There are various useful built-in functions in Python that can be used with lists.

`listLength = len(playerName)` will assign 5, the number of items in the list, to `listLength`

Look at the array code above.
  (a) How would you refer to the name "Lennie"?
  (b) Write a statement to print the last name in the list.
  (c) The statement `index = int((len(playerName))/2)` assigns the integer part of the division by 2 to `index`.
     What will be printed by the statement: `print(playerName(index)`
  (d) Write an algorithm to swap the names "Corrie" and "Ben" in the list.

  (a) *playerName[3]*   (b) *print(playerName[4])*   (c) *Gordon*

  (d) *temp = playerName[0]*
     playerName[0] = playerName[1]
     playerName[1] = temp

TRACE TABLES

A **trace table** is used to show how the values of variables change during execution of a program.

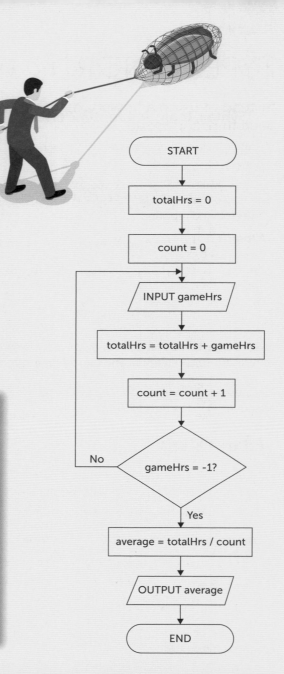

As each line of code is executed, the current value of any variable or logical expression that is changed is written in the appropriate column of the table below. It is not necessary to fill in a cell if the value has not changed from the line above.

Example: Ben designs a flowchart for an algorithm to calculate the average number of hours students spend per week playing computer games. He uses test data for 3 students spending respectively 8, 10 and 12 hours playing games. This should result in an average of 10 hours.

A trace table, shown below, has identified an error with the flowchart.

Describe how the algorithm could be corrected.   [3]

The input, gameHrs, should be tested right after it has been input.[1] However, a program cannot jump out of a loop before completing it.[1] Therefore, the input statement and the test for gameHrs = −1 should be placed at the end of the loop.[1] An initial input statement is required before entering the loop.[1]

Download the Python program **Sec 1.2 Trace table game hrs corrected.py** from **www.clearrevise.com**

gameHrs	totalHrs	count	gameHrs = −1?	average
	0	0		
8	8	1	No	
10	18	2	No	
12	30	3	No	
−1	29	4	Yes	7.25

Oops! The algorithm must be incorrect, since it produces the wrong answer.

TYPES OF ERROR

Syntax, logic and runtime errors

There are three types of error that may prevent a program from working correctly, or from running at all.

A **syntax error** will prevent your program from running. It is typically caused by a mistake in the spelling or 'grammar' of your code. For example `primt("Hello World")`. Syntax errors will be detected and reported by the compiler or interpreter.

A **logic error** is harder to spot. Your program will run but may crash or give an incorrect or unexpected output. Common examples involve the use of greater than or less than symbols, for example: using `x > 5` instead of `x >= 5` which could affect loop conditions or range checks. Another example of a common logic error is missing brackets in mathematics calculations, e.g.:

```
VAT = (orderTotal - discount) * taxRate  gives a different answer to:
VAT = orderTotal - discount * taxRate
```

Using a well thought-out test plan, with the expected results manually calculated first, should reveal any logic errors. Using a trace table may help to find and correct the errors.

A **runtime error** is one which will be detected when the program is run. It may be caused by a logic error, erroneous user input, or by the program not allowing for a condition such as a user inputting zero, or entering no data at all. Division by zero will also cause a runtime error.

---

1. Look at the following Python code.
```
total = 0
x = 0
while x != 100:
    total = total + x
    x = x + 3
print("total = ",x)
```
   (a) Explain what will happen when the code is executed. [2]

   (b) What type of error causes this to happen? [1]

2. The code below is intended to add the even numbers between 1 and 50.
```
count = 0
while count <= 50:
    count = count + 2
    sum = sum + count
print(Total:, sum)
```
   Find **three** errors in this code. State in each case whether they are syntax, logic or runtime errors. [6]

   1. (a) *x will never be 100[1], so the program will run in an infinite loop[1].*

      (b) This is a runtime error[1] caused by a logic error[1] in the program.

   2. *sum has not been initialised.[1] This is a logic error[1] which will cause a runtime error.[1]*
      count <= 50 will cause the number 52 to be included, as the while condition is not checked until all the statements in the loop have been executed. Two statements within the while loop should be swapped.[1] Logic error.[1] print(Total:, sum) doesn't have the string in quote marks.[1] It should be: print("Total:", sum)[1]. Syntax error.[1]

SEARCHING ALGORITHMS

Binary search

A binary search can be used to search a list that is in numerical or alphabetical order. It works by repeatedly dividing in half the portion of the list that could contain the required data item.

Example: An ordered list of 12 numbers contains the following data items. To find whether the number 37 is in the list, start by examining the middle item in the list. This is the sixth item in this list of 12 numbers.

25	26	28	37	39	40	41	43	56	70	74	81

Stage 1: The middle item is 40. The search item 37 is less than 40. Discard all the items greater than or equal to 40.

25	26	28	37	39

Stage 2: The middle item is the third item, which is 28. 37 is greater than 28, so discard items less than or equal to 28.

37	39

Stage 3: The 'middle' item in a list of two numbers is the first one 37. This is the number we are searching for, so the algorithm can report that the number has been found. If we had been searching for, say, 36, we would know at this stage that the number is not in the list.

37

Sometimes the search item is found before completing all stages. If the search had been for the number 40, we would have found it at Stage 1, its position in the list would be returned and the algorithm could then be made to terminate.

Linear search

In a linear search, each item will be checked one by one in the list. This is very slow for large lists, but necessary if the list is not sorted. For large, sorted lists, a binary search is much more efficient as the number of items to be examined is halved at each stage.

A list of 14 names is shown below.

Anne	Bob	Chas	Eric	Fiona	Harry	Jo	Ken	Mona	Nahim	Geri	Peter	Steve	Zoe

(a) State which items are examined when looking for **Steve** using a binary search. [2]

(b) State which items are examined when looking for **Dave** using a binary search. [4]

(c) State how many items will be examined when looking for **Dave** in the list of names using a linear search. [1]

(a) Jo[1], Geri[1], (Steve will be the next search item).

(b) Jo[1], Chas[1], Fiona[1], Eric[1], (name not found).

(c) 14[1]

COMPARING AND CONTRASTING SEARCH ALGORITHMS

Binary search	Linear search
| ```
#Binary search
aList = [2, 3, 11, 12, 15, 19, 23, 30, 36, 45]
OUTPUT("List to be searched:", aList)
found = False
first = 0
last = LEN(aList) - 1
searchItem = USERINPUT
WHILE NOT found AND first ≤ last
    midpt = REAL_TO_INT((first+last) / 2)
    IF aList[midpt] == searchItem THEN
        found = True
        index = midpt
    ELSE
        IF aList[midpt] < searchItem THEN
            first = midpt + 1
        ELSE
            last = midpt - 1
        ENDIF
    ENDIF
ENDWHILE
IF found THEN
    OUTPUT("Found at position", index,
        "in the list")
ELSE
    OUTPUT("Item is not in the list")
ENDIF
``` | ```
#Linear search
aList = [14, 2, 3, 11, 1, 9, 5, 8, 10, 6]
OUTPUT("List to be searched:", aList)
found = False
index = 0
searchItem = USERINPUT
WHILE NOT found AND index < LEN(aList)
    IF aList[index] == searchItem THEN
        found = True
    ELSE
        index = index + 1
    ENDIF
ENDWHILE
IF found THEN
    OUTPUT(searchItem, "in position",
        index, "of the list")
ELSE
    OUTPUT("Item not found")
ENDIF
```  |

Linear search vs binary search

In a list of 1 million items, on average it will be necessary to examine 500,000 items to find a given item using a linear search. Using a binary search, only 20 items would need to be examined in a list of 1,000,000 items to find an item or to conclude that it is not in the list!

Give **two** reasons why you would use a linear search to find an item in a list. [2]

If the list is unsorted, it is not possible to do a binary search[1], so a linear sort must be performed. On a very short list, the execution time for a linear search and a binary search is not significant[1] and a linear search is a simpler algorithm[1].

Use the pseudocode given above to write Python programs to perform binary and linear searches.

Download the completed Python programs **Sec 1.2 Binary search.py** and **Sec 1.2 Linear search.py** from **www.clearrevise.com**.

BUBBLE SORT

A bubble sort works by repeatedly going through the list to be sorted, swapping adjacent elements if they are in the wrong order.

To sort a list of n items, a maximum of n–1 passes is required. (The items may be alphabetical or numeric.)

Example

A list of 5 numbers 7, 3, 5, 9, 4 is to be sorted. Show the state of the list after each pass.

List	7	3	5	9	4	

Pass 1	3	7	5	9	4	
	3	5	7	9	4	
	3	5	7	9	4	
	3	5	7	4	9	Examine 5 items

After the first pass through the list, the largest number has 'bubbled' to the end of the list. In the second pass, we only need to compare the first four items.

Pass 2	3	5	7	4	9	
	3	5	7	4	9	
	3	5	4	7	9	Examine 4 items

Pass 3	3	5	4	7	9	
	3	4	5	7	9	Examine 3 items

Pass 4	3	4	5	7	9	Examine 2 items

The list is now sorted.

The list of animals **hamster, rabbit, dog, cat, goldfish**, is to be sorted in alphabetical order using a bubble sort. Show the state of the list after:

(a) Pass 1   [1]

(b) Pass 2   [1]

(a) hamster, dog, cat, goldfish, rabbit[1]

(b) dog, cat, goldfish, hamster, rabbit[1]

The bubble sort algorithm is not efficient for large lists. Note that in some cases, the algorithm may have sorted the list before performing the full number of passes. If no swaps are made during a particular pass, then the list must already be sorted. This condition could be tested and the algorithm could be made to terminate.

The algorithm for the bubble sort, including this modification, is given on page 12.

MERGE SORT

This is a very fast two-stage sort. In the first stage, the list is successively divided in half, forming two sublists, until each sublist is of length one.

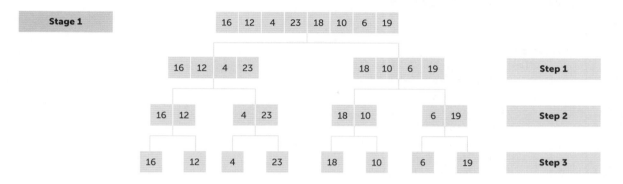

At the end of stage 1, all the elements have been separated out.

In the second stage, each pair of sublists is repeatedly merged to produce new sorted sublists until there is only one sublist remaining. This is the sorted list.

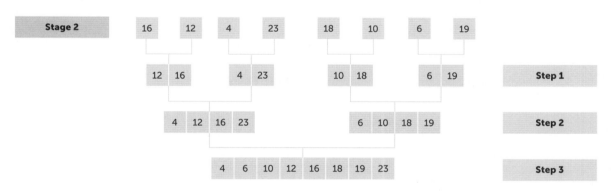

1. Write the list that results from merging the two lists 2, 5, 17, 38, 56 and 3, 4, 15, 19, 36 [1]

2. The following list is to be sorted using a merge sort algorithm.

Giraffe	Zebra	Monkey	Leopard	Hippo	Warthog	Rhino

(a) Describe the two stages of a merge sort algorithm. [4]

(b) Write out the list after Step 2 of the Stage 2 process. [2]

1. The list would be: 2, 3, 4, 5, 15, 17, 19, 36, 38, 56[1]

2. (a) Stage 1: The list is successively divided in half[1], forming two sublists[1], until each sublist is of length one[1].

   Stage 2: Each pair of sublists[1] is repeatedly merged[1] to produce new sorted sublists[1] until there is only one list remaining[1].

   (b) Giraffe, Leopard, Monkey, Zebra,[1]   Hippo, Rhino, Warthog[1]

COMPARING BUBBLE SORT AND MERGE SORT

Bubble sort vs Merge sort

The algorithm for the bubble sort is given below.

```
01  #Sec 1.2 Bubble sort with flag
02  aList = [17, 3, 7, 15, 13, 23, 20]
03  #Get number of items in the array
04  numItems = len(aList)
05  comparisons = numItems - 1
06  swapMade = True
07  while comparisons > 0 and swapMade:
08     swapMade = False
09     for j in range(comparisons):
10        if aList[j] > aList[j + 1]:
11           temp = aList[j]
12           aList[j] = aList[j + 1]
13           aList[j + 1] = temp
14           swapMade = True
15     comparisons = comparisons - 1
16  print("Sorted list:",aList)
```

The Merge Sort algorithm is a more complex, **recursive** algorithm, meaning that it uses a subroutine that calls itself. (Recursion is beyond the scope of this course.)

The Bubble Sort algorithm, on the other hand, is an **iterative** algorithm, meaning that it uses WHILE and/or FOR loops, repeating the same steps many times.

For small data sets, the difference in execution time for each of these sorts will be insignificant. However, for very large data sets, the merge sort is many times faster. A bubble sort could take several hours to sort a data set that a merge sort would sort in a few minutes or even seconds.

Look at the bubble sort algorithm above.

(a) State the line numbers of the Bubble Sort code given above which swaps two items in the list. [1]

(b) State the purpose of the variable named `temp`. [1]

(c) Explain the purpose of the variable named `swapMade`. [3]

> *(a) 11, 12, 13.[1]*
>
> *(b) `temp` is used to temporarily store the value of one of the variables to be swapped[1]. When the second value overwrites it, the value can be moved from `temp` into the second variable[1].*
>
> *(c) This is used to indicate when two values are swapped[1]. If `swapMade` is false, this shows that no values were swapped in a pass and the WHILE loop will then terminate[1] instead of doing more unnecessary passes[1]. This is a more efficient algorithm than one that always performs the full number of passes.*

Download the Python program **Sec 1.2 Bubble sort with flag.py** from **www.clearrevise.com**.

EFFICIENCY OF ALGORITHMS

The efficiency of an algorithm can be measured by the time it takes to execute, or the amount of memory required for a given dataset. Execution time depends on the number of compares, and/or the number of passes through a loop.

This course examines two algorithms for searching a list, and two algorithms for sorting a list. In each case, one algorithm is much more efficient than the other.

A **merge sort**, for example, will sort a large number of items in a fraction of the time taken by a **bubble sort**.

A **binary search** will find an item in a long list of sorted items, or discover that it is not in the list, in a fraction of the time taken by a **linear search**.

Example

Here is an algorithm that prints "Name is in the list" if a particular name is found in a list of 1,000 unsorted names. The names are held in a list named **aList**, and the first name is referred to as **aList[0]**.

```
nameSought = input("Enter name sought: ")
nameFound = False
for index in range(1000):
    if aList[index] == nameSought:
        nameFound = True
if nameFound:
    print("Name is in the list")
else:
    print("Name not found")
```

1. Look at the Python code provided on the left.

   Explain why this is an inefficient algorithm. [2]

   It is inefficient because even if the name is found right at the beginning of the list[1], the algorithm continues searching every item in the list[1]. It needs to terminate as soon as the item is found.[1]

Many problems, both simple and complex, have more than one method of solution. Consider the problem of finding the sum of the integers from 1 to n.

Here are two different algorithms for solving the problem:

Algorithm 1:	Algorithm 2:

`n = input("Enter final integer")`
`total = 0`
`for index in range(1, n+1):`
`    total = total + index`
	`n = input("Enter final integer")`
	`total = n * (n + 1)/2`

In the second algorithm, only one instruction is needed to find the total.

2. How many times is the loop executed in Algorithm 1 if the user inputs 1,000,000? [1]

   1,000,000.[1]

TRUTH TABLES

Simple logic gates

The electronic circuits in a computer are constructed from **logic gates** which can only be in one of two states: on or off, 1 or 0. Three simple logic gates are shown below. Each is represented by a diagram and a truth table showing the possible outputs for each possible input.

AND gate (*Conjunction*)   **OR** gate (*Disjunction*)   **NOT** gate (*Negation*)

 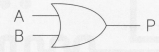 

AND		
A	B	P = A AND B
0	0	0
0	1	0
1	0	0
1	1	1

OR		
A	B	P = A OR B
0	0	0
0	1	1
1	0	1
1	1	1

NOT	
A	P = NOT A
0	1
1	0

Logic gates can be combined to produce more complicated circuits. This circuit can be represented by the logic statement: P = (A AND B) OR (NOT B).

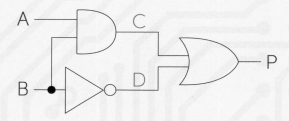

The truth table is given below.

A	B	C (A AND B)	D (NOT B)	P (C OR D)
0	0	0	1	1
0	1	0	0	0
1	0	0	1	1
1	1	1	0	1

1. Draw a truth table giving all possible inputs for A, B and C, and output P, corresponding to the logic statement P = (A AND NOT B) OR C. [4]

2. A logic circuit is being developed for a bus shelter advert that plays automatically if a passenger is detected in or around the bus stop.

- The system has two sensors, S1 and S2, that detect if a passenger is near. The advert plays if either of these sensors is activated.
- The advert should only play if it is not daytime (D).
- The output from the circuit, for whether the advert should play or not, is P.

   (a) Write the logic statement for this system. [2]

   (b) Complete the truth table for this system. [4]

S1	S2	D	S1 OR S2	NOT D	P
0	0	0			
0	0	1			
0	1				
0	1				
1					
1					
1					
1					

1.

A	B	C	NOT B [1]	D = A AND NOT B [1]	P = D OR C [2]
0	0	0	1	0	0
0	0	1	1	0	1
0	1	0	0	0	0
0	1	1	0	0	1
1	0	0	1	1	1
1	0	1	1	1	1
1	1	0	0	0	0
1	1	1	0	0	1

2. (a) P = (S1 OR S2)[1] AND NOT D[1]

   (b)

S1	S2	D	S1 OR S2 [1]	NOT D [1]	P [2]
0	0	0	0	1	0
0	0	1	0	0	0
0	1	0	1	1	1
0	1	1	1	0	0
1	0	0	1	1	1
1	0	1	1	0	0
1	1	0	1	1	1
1	1	1	1	0	0

EXAMINATION PRACTICE

1. An algorithm is given below.

```
01   array aList = [3,6,7,9,13,15,16,19,20,24,26,29,36]
02   found = False
03   n = 0
04   x = input("Enter a number: ")
05   while found == False and n < len(aList):
06     if aList[n] == x:
07             found = True
08             print(x, "found at position ", n)
09     else:
10             n = n + 1
11   if not found:
12     print("Invalid number")
```

(a) Explain the purpose of this algorithm. [2]

(b) At line 05, what is the value of `len(aList)`? [1]

(c) The user enters 9 at line 04. How many times is the **while** loop performed? [1]

(d) Explain how the use of the variable named **found** makes the algorithm more efficient. [2]

2. An array **names** holds **n** items. An algorithm for a bubble sort is given below.

```
01   swapMade = True
02   while swapMade
03     swapMade = False
04     for index = 0 to n - 2
05       if names[index] > names[index+1] then
06               swap the names
07               swapMade = True
08       endif
09     next index
10   endwhile
```

(a) Explain the purpose of the variable swapMade in the algorithm. [2]

(b) Write the code for "*swap the names*" in line 06. [3]

(c) The list **names** contains the following:

Edna   Adam   Victor   Charlie   Jack   Ken   Maria

Write the contents of the list after each of the first two times the **while…endwhile** loop
is executed. [2]

(d) How many times will the **while** loop be executed before the program terminates?
Explain your answer. [2]

3. An algorithm is given below.

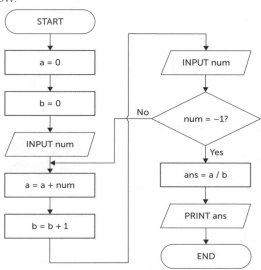

(a) Complete the trace table to show how the variables change, and what will be output, if the numbers 3, 8, 2, 5, −1 are entered. [4]

num	a	b	ans
	0	0	
3	3	1	
8			

(b) State the purpose of the algorithm. [1]

4. Complete the truth table corresponding to the following logic statement:

X = NOT(A OR B) OR (B AND C) [4]

A	B	C	Working space	X
0	0	0		
0	0	1		
0	1	0		
0	1	1		

BINARY REPRESENTATION

Bit 0 or 1	Nibble 4 Bits	Byte 8 Bits	Kibibyte (KiB) 1024 Bytes	Mebibyte (MiB) 1024 KiB	Gibibyte (GiB) 1024 MiB	Tebibyte (TiB) 1024 GiB

A computer is made up of billions of **switches**, each with two states - an **off** position (represented by a 0) and an **on** position (represented by a 1). This is known as **binary**. All data therefore needs to be converted into binary before it can be processed by a computer.

With two or more switches, the number of combinations of 1s and 0s is doubled with each additional switch or **bit**.

Computers use binary to represent everything including numbers, text, sound, graphics and program instructions. The number of binary digits (or switches) used determines the number of states that can be represented.

Number of switches	Expression	Possible combinations of states
1	2^1	2
2	2^2	4
3	2^3	8
4	2^4	16
5	2^5	32
6	2^6	64
7	2^7	128
8	2^8	256

8 switches or bits each have two possible states. An 8-bit byte has 2x2x2x2x2x2x2x2 or 2^8 = 256 possible states, or combinations of bits, from 0000 0000 to 1111 1111.

Calculate the following:

(a) Calculate the number of 650 MiB CDs required to store 2 GiB of images. Show your working. [1]

(b) Calculate in TiB the total capacity of a server with 4 × 2.5 TiB hard disk drives. [1]

(c) Calculate the total storage requirement for a database of 5,000 customer records each of 1.5 kiB each. Give your answer in MiB. Show your working. [2]

(d) Calculate the maximum number of states that can be represented in a binary pattern of 10 bits. [1]

(a) 2 GiB = 2048 MiB. 2048/650 = 3.15 (>3). Therefore 4 CDs will be required.[1]

(b) 10 TiB.[1]

(c) 5000 × 1.5 kiB = 7500 kiB.[1] = 7.32 MiB.[1]

(d) 10 bits, each with 2 combinations = 2^{10} = 1024.[1]

BINARY ⇄ DENARY CONVERSION

Converting binary numbers into positive denary whole numbers

Our denary or decimal system has a base of 10 digits 0–9. Binary has a base of just 2 digits, 0 and 1. Instead of a representing three-digit numbers with a ones, tens and hundreds column for example, binary represents them with a ones column, a twos column and a fours column.

To make a conversion from binary to denary, add the place value headers where there is a 1.

128	64	32	16	8	4	2	1
0	1	1	0	1	0	0	1
	1×64 +	1×32 +		1×8 +			1×1 = 105

Converting positive denary whole numbers to binary

To convert the denary number 87 into binary, start with the **most significant bit** (left-hand end of the table below). Does 128 go into 87? If not, add a 0 in that column. Does 64 go into 87? Yes, it does, so add a 1 to the column and calculate the remainder, 23. 32 does not go into 23 so add a 0 to the next column. 16 goes into 23 with a remainder of 7. 8 won't go into 7 so add a 0 next. 4 will go with a remainder of 3. 2 will go into 3 with a remainder of 1 and 1 goes into 1 so add a 1 to each of the last three columns.

Note that the maximum value that can be held with eight bits where all bits = 1, is 255.

A binary number with a 1 in the least significant bit (far right-hand position) will always be odd.

128	64	32	16	8	4	2	1
0	1	0	1	0	1	1	1
	r23		r7		r3	r1	

1. Convert the following denary numbers to binary:
   (a) 138 [1]
   (b) 57 [1]
2. Convert the following binary numbers to denary:
   (a) 0110 1101 [1]
   (b) 1110 0110 [1]

   1. (a) 1000 1010[1], (b) 0011 1001[1]
   2. (a) 109[1], (b) 230[1]

Counting in binary

0	0000		8	1000
1	0001		9	1001
2	0010		10	1010
3	0011		11	1011
4	0100		12	1100
5	0101		13	1101
6	0110		14	1110
7	0111		15	1111

TWO'S COMPLEMENT SIGNED INTEGERS

An **unsigned** representation of a binary number can only represent positive numbers. A **signed** integer can represent both positive and negative numbers.

Two's complement

Using two's complement, the leftmost bit is the **sign bit**. If it is 1, the number is negative. If it is 0, the number is positive.

Two's complement works in a similar way to numbers on an analogue counter. When it shows 0000, moving the wheel forwards by one, would create a reading of 0001. Moving it backwards would create a reading of 9999, which is interpreted as −1.

1111 1101	=	−3
1111 1110	=	−2
1111 1111	=	−1
0000 0000	=	0
0000 0001	=	1
0000 0010	=	2
0000 0011	=	3

The maximum range that can be represented with 8 bits is −128 to 127 because the leftmost bit is used as the sign bit, with a value of −128, leaving only 7 bits to represent the positive part of the number. A 1 as the leftmost bit indicates the number is negative.

In an 8-bit byte, the leftmost bit represents = −128

Converting a negative denary number to binary

Work out the positive binary equivalent of the number, flip all of the bits and add 1.

For example:
Target: −21
Positive 21: 0001 0101
Flip the bits: 1110 1010
Add one: 1
Convert: 1110 1011

Converting a negative two's complement binary number to denary

The same method works the other way. Flip all of the bits and add 1. Then work out the denary equivalent as normal.

For example:
Target: 1110 1110
Flip the bits: 0001 0001
Add one: 1
Convert: −0001 0010   = −18

1. Convert the following denary numbers to signed binary integers:
   (a) −128 [1]   (b) −57 [1]   (c) −9 [1]
2. Convert the following signed binary integers to denary:
   (a) 1000 0011 [1]   (b) 1110 0110 [1]   (c) 1110 0101 [1]
   1. (a) 1000 0000[1], (b) 1100 0111[1], (c) 1111 0111[1]   2. (a) −125[1], (b) −26[1], (c) −27[1]

ADDING POSITIVE UNSIGNED BINARY INTEGERS

Binary addition is done in the same way that denary numbers might be added together.

The rules are as follows:

> 0 + 0 = 0
> 0 + 1 or 1 + 0 = 1
> 1 + 1 = 0 carry a 1
> 1 + 1 + 1 = 1 carry a 1

Note that in the same way as the denary values 00028 and 28 represent the same value, the binary value 00011100 is the same as 11100. Any leading zeros (left-hand side) are ignored.

Carry	1	1	1	1		1			Check
	0	1	0	1	1	0	1	1	91
+	0	0	1	1	1	0	1	0	58
	1	0	0	1	0	1	0	1	149

Overflow

Overflow occurs when the result of adding two binary numbers is greater than the number of bits allowed, (eight in this example). The maximum value that can be held with 8 bits is 255. (In practice, integers would be held typically in 32 bits.)

Consider the following example to illustrate this:

1						1	1		Check
	1	1	0	0	0	0	0	1	193
+	1	0	0	0	1	0	1	1	139
1	0	1	0	0	1	1	0	0	332

If a binary number represents an 8-bit two's complement number rather than an unsigned integer, overflow will occur when the result of a calculation is greater than 127.

1. Add the following binary numbers, leaving the answer as binary numbers.
   (a) 0011 1011 + 1000 0110 [1]
   (b) 1001 1100 + 0111 1110 [1]
2. Explain the problem that would occur in part 1(b) if the result was to be stored as an 8-bit number. [2]

   1. (a) 1100 0001[1], (b) 1 0001 1010[1]

   2. Overflow error[1] since the total was more than 11111111[1] (255 in denary.)

BINARY SHIFTS

There are two types of binary shift – a **logical** shift and an **arithmetic** shift.

Logical shift

A logical shift moves all of the bits in a given binary number either to the left or the right by a given number of places. All of the empty spaces are then filled with zeros.

A shift of one place to the left will have the following effect:

A shift of three places to the right will result in the following:

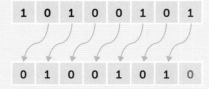 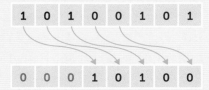

Arithmetic shift

A **left arithmetic shift** is identical to a **left logical shift**.

The result of a left shift is to multiply the number by 2^n, where n is the number of places shifted. However, if the leftmost bit (the sign bit) is changed by the shift, **overflow** results.

With a **right arithmetic shift** of one place, each bit moves right one place. The rightmost bit is discarded and the leftmost bit is filled with the previous value, which has been shifted right. This preserves the sign bit. Each shift right divides the number by 2. There may be a loss of precision. (e.g. 13 ÷ 2 = 6.5, but a shift right of 00001101 results in 00000110, i.e. 6.)

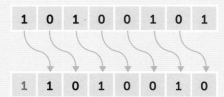

In a right arithmetic shift, the least significant bit is discarded and the vacant leftmost bit (the sign bit) is filled with the value of the bit previously in that position, preserving the sign bit.

1. Explain the effect of a 2-place left logical shift on the signed binary number 0001 0110 [1]
2. Explain the effect of a 1-place right arithmetic shift on the signed binary number 1010 1111 [2]
3. Explain the effect of a 2-place left arithmetic shift on the signed binary number 0110 1101 [2]

   1. *Result is 0101 1000. The number is multiplied by 4.[1]*

   2. *Result is 1101 0111. The sign bit is preserved and the number is divided by $2^{[1]}$, with loss of precision[1]. The original value −81 is divided by 2, but gives the value −41, rather than −40.5.*

   3. *1011 0100. Overflow has occurred[1], changing the value[1] and sign from positive to negative.[1]*

HEXADECIMAL ⇄ BINARY CONVERSION

The **hexadecimal** number system uses a base of 16 instead of 2 or 10. Given that we only have ten digits 0–9 in our system, the additional six number 10–15 in the hexadecimal system are represented by the letters A–F.

Denary	Binary	Hex
0	0000	0
1	0001	1
2	0010	2
3	0011	3
4	0100	4
5	0101	5
6	0110	6
7	0111	7

Denary	Binary	Hex
8	1000	8
9	1001	9
10	1010	A
11	1011	B
12	1100	C
13	1101	D
14	1110	E
15	1111	F

One hexadecimal (or hex) number can represent one nibble of 4 bits. This is easier to remember than the binary representation.

Converting a binary number into hexadecimal

To convert the number 0100 1111 to hexadecimal, first split the eight-bit binary number into two nibbles of four bits each. Convert each nibble separately and join the results.

0100	1111	=	01001111
4	15 (F)		4F

Some further examples are:
1011 0101 = **B5** and 1100 1101 = **CD**

Converting a hexadecimal number into binary

Convert each hex character into a four-bit binary value and join them to make a byte.

7	E (14)	=	7E
0111	1110		01111110

Further examples are: B9 = 1011 1001 and DA = 1101 1010.

1. Convert the following binary values into hexadecimal: [3]
   (a) 0110 1011
   (b) 0000 1001
   (c) 1111 1111
2. Convert the following hexadecimal values into binary: [3]
   (a) 48
   (b) 6A
   (c) F9

1. (a) 6B[1], (b) 09[1], (c) FF[1]
2. (a) 0100 1000[1], (b) 0110 1010[1], (c) 1111 1001[1]

To convert between hexadecimal and denary, you can convert via binary.

USES OF HEXADECIMAL

Hexadecimal numbers are easier to read and remember than binary, so they are used in the following situations:

- Colour values in photo editing software and HTML
- MAC addresses
- Memory address locations in assembly language

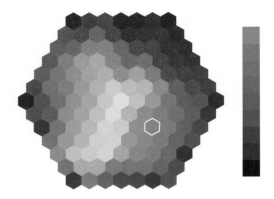

Hexadecimal colour number: ED468C

CHARACTER ENCODING

Each character on a keyboard has a binary code which is transmitted to the computer each time a key is pressed.

Some of the characters and their codes, known as the **character set**, for the standard keyboard are given opposite. The **ASCII** character set consists of 128 characters, each using 7 bits to uniquely represent them. ASCII stands for American Standard Code for Information Interchange. Extended ASCII uses 8 bits (or 1 byte) per character.

Use the ASCII table opposite for this question.

(a) Show how the word CAGE is represented in 7-bit ASCII. Give your answer in binary. [1]

(b) One byte is used to store one character. The leftmost bit of each byte is set to 0. State how many bytes would be used to store the phrase "BIRD CAGE". [1]

(c) The uppercase character 'T' in ASCII is represented by the denary value 84. State the denary value for the character 'R'. [1]

(a) 1000011 1000001 1000111 1000101[1]

(b) 9 bytes.[1] (The Space character has the denary code 32 and occupies one byte.)

(c) 'R' is 82.[1]

7-bit ASCII table

ASCII	DEC	Binary	ASCII	DEC	Binary	ASCII	DEC	Binary	ASCII	DEC	Binary
NULL	000	000 0000	space	032	010 0000	@	064	100 0000	`	096	110 0000
SOH	001	000 0001	!	033	010 0001	A	065	100 0001	a	097	110 0001
STX	002	000 0010	"	034	010 0010	B	066	100 0010	b	098	110 0010
ETX	003	000 0011	#	035	010 0011	C	067	100 0011	c	099	110 0011
EOT	004	000 0100	$	036	010 0100	D	068	100 0100	d	100	110 0100
ENQ	005	000 0101	%	037	010 0101	E	069	100 0101	e	101	110 0101
ACK	006	000 0110	&	038	010 0110	F	070	100 0110	f	102	110 0110
BEL	007	000 0111	'	039	010 0111	G	071	100 0111	g	103	110 0111
BS	008	000 1000	(	040	010 1000	H	072	100 1000	h	104	110 1000
HT	009	000 1001	)	041	010 1001	I	073	100 1001	i	105	110 1001
LF	010	000 1010	*	042	010 1010	J	074	100 1010	j	106	110 1010
VT	011	000 1011	+	043	010 1011	K	075	100 1011	k	107	110 1011
FF	012	000 1100	,	044	010 1100	L	076	100 1100	l	108	110 1100
CR	013	000 1101	-	045	010 1101	M	077	100 1101	m	109	110 1101
SO	014	000 1110	.	046	010 1110	N	078	100 1110	n	110	110 1110
SI	015	000 1111	/	047	010 1111	O	079	100 1111	o	111	110 1111
DLE	016	001 0000	0	048	011 0000	P	080	101 0000	p	112	111 0000
DC1	017	001 0001	1	049	011 0001	Q	081	101 0001	q	113	111 0001
DC2	018	001 0010	2	050	011 0010	R	082	101 0010	r	114	111 0010
DC3	019	001 0011	3	051	011 0011	S	083	101 0011	s	115	111 0011
DC4	020	001 0100	4	052	011 0100	T	084	101 0100	t	116	111 0100
NAK	021	001 0101	5	053	011 0101	U	085	101 0101	u	117	111 0101
SYN	022	001 0110	6	054	011 0110	V	086	101 0110	v	118	111 0110
ETB	023	001 0111	7	055	011 0111	W	087	101 0111	w	119	111 0111
CAN	024	001 1000	8	056	011 1000	X	088	101 1000	x	120	111 1000
EM	025	001 1001	9	057	011 1001	Y	089	101 1001	y	121	111 1001
SUB	026	001 1010	:	058	011 1010	Z	090	101 1010	z	122	111 1010
ESC	027	001 1011	;	059	011 1011	[	091	101 1011	{	123	111 1011
FS	028	001 1100	<	060	011 1100	\	092	101 1100			124	111 1100
GS	029	001 1101	=	061	011 1101	]	093	101 1101	}	125	111 1101
RS	030	001 1110	>	062	011 1110	^	094	101 1110	~	126	111 1110
US	031	001 1111	?	063	011 1111	_	095	101 1111	DEL	127	111 1111

Using the ASCII table in programming

The character codes are grouped and run in sequence; e.g. given that uppercase 'A' is 65 then 'B' must be 66 and so on. The pattern applies to other groupings such as lowercase characters and digits. For example, '1' is 49, so '5' must be 53. Also, '3' < '4' and 'a' < 'b'.

Notice that the ASCII code value for '7' (011 0111) is different from the pure binary value for 7 (000 0111). This is why you can't calculate with numbers that have been input as strings.

REPRESENTING IMAGES

Similar to a mosaic, a **bitmap** image is made up of picture elements or **pixels**. A pixel represents the smallest identifiable area of an image, each appearing as a square of a single colour.

Colour depth

The first symbol below is represented in black and white using a series of binary codes. 0 = black and 1 = white.

0	1	1	1
1	0	1	0
1	1	0	0
1	0	0	0

11	11	11	00
10	10	10	10
10	10	01	10
10	10	01	10

Given that only 1 bit per pixel is available, only two colours, black and white, can be represented. The full image would have a size of 16 bits or 2 bytes. If the number of bits per pixel is increased, more colours can be represented. In the second example, four colours can be represented as the **colour depth** (also known as **bit depth**, or bits per pixel) has been doubled to two. This will also double the file size.

Image size

The size of an image is expressed as width × height of the image in pixels, for example 600 × 400px.

Number of colours		Colour depth
2 colours	2^1 colours	1 bit per pixel required
4 colours	2^2 colours	2 bits per pixel required
8 colours	2^3 colours	3 bits per pixel required
16 colours	2^4 colours	4 bits per pixel required

---

1. Study the bitmap images above.

   (a) Give the binary representation for the top row of the 4-colour example. [2]

   (b) State the colour depth of an image if a palette of 256 colours per pixel is required. [1]

   The number of available colours in the 4 x 4 pixel image above is increased to 256.

   (c) State the effect on the file size of the image. [1]

   > (a) 11 11[1] 11 00[1]. One mark per correct pair.
   >
   > (b) 8 bits per pixel.[1] ($2^8 = 256$)
   >
   > (c) The file size would increase[1] to 1 byte per pixel, i.e. 16 bytes for the whole image[1].

Effect of colour depth and resolution

As the number of bits per pixel increases (the **colour depth** or **bit depth**), so does the quality of the image as you are able to more accurately represent the full range of colours visible to the naked eye. However, this significantly increases the **file size**.

| *2 colours* | *4 colours* | *8 colours* | *16 colours* | *256 colours* | *65.536 colours* | *16.7m colours* |

The file size of an image in bits can be calculated as *width in pixels x height in pixels x colour depth*. Dividing by 8 will give the size in bytes.

Simply increasing the number of pixels in an image will also increase its size. An 8 x 8 pixel icon will be four times larger than a 4 x 4 pixel icon with the same colour depth.

| 1 × 1 | 2 × 2 | 5 × 5 | 10 × 10 | 25 × 25 | 50 × 50 | 72 × 72 | 300 × 300 |

The density of pixels in the same sized area defines the **resolution**. More pixels per inch (**PPI**) will smooth the edges and improve the overall quality. This will increase the size of the image file, making it possible to enlarge the image without a visible loss of quality. Improved resolution, however, comes at the expense of either increasing the number of pixels in an image (increasing file size) or reducing the pixel size and therefore the visible size of the image.

---

2. An image has 1024 x 1024 pixels and a colour depth of 24 bits.

(a) State the file size in MiB. [2]

(b) Write an expression to show how many colours are available for each pixel if an image has a colour depth of 24 bits. [1]

(a) 1024 × 1024 × 24 / 8.[1] = 3 MiB.[1]

(b) 2^{24} = 16,777,216 = 16.7m colours.[1]

SOUND

Analogue sounds must be digitally recorded in binary. In order to record sound, the **amplitude** or height of the soundwave emitted must be measured and recorded at regular intervals. How often the height is recorded (the **frequency** or **sample rate**), and the accuracy to which the height is recorded (the **bit depth** or **sample resolution**) affect the quality of the recorded sound when played back and the file size of the recording. The **duration** of the recording will also affect the file size.

The **sample rate** is measured in **hertz**. CD quality playback is recorded at 44.1 KHz.

Examples A and B show how the digitally represented wave more accurately follows the analogue sound wave form with a greater **bit depth**.

Examples B and C show how waves recorded at identical resolutions are much more accurately represented with a greater number of **samples per second**.

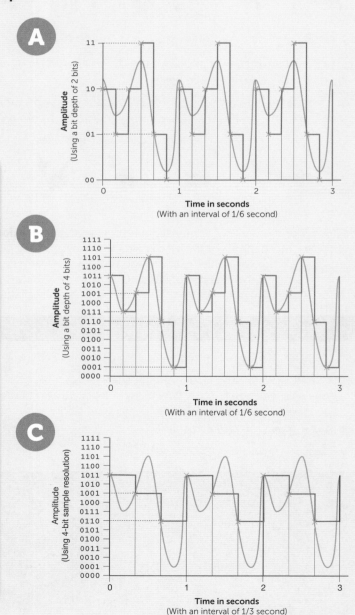

Look at Examples A, B and C.

(a) Give the binary representation for the first six samples taken in the first second of recording in Example A. [2]

(b) State how many different amplitudes or wave heights could be recorded if the bit depth was 8. [1]

(c) State the sample frequency in hertz of Example C. [1]

(d) Calculate the file size in bytes of a message alert tone lasting 3 seconds, using a sample rate of 8 kHz and an 8-bit sample resolution. [1]

(a) 10, 01, 10[1], 11, 01, 00[1]

(b) 2^8 = 256[1]

(c) 3 Hz[1] (3 samples per second.)

(d) 8,000 samples per second, taken at 8 bits each = 64 kilobits / 8 = 8 kB x 3 seconds duration = 24 kB.[1]

COMPRESSION

Compression software uses **algorithms** to remove repeated or unnecessary data. This reduces the size of a file on disk, and of large files sent by email where there are maximum attachment limits. It is also useful for streaming data over the Internet and for images and video embedded within websites as smaller files will be transmitted in less time, meaning the streamed video content or website takes less time to download. A **bitmap** (**.bmp**) image is uncompressed.

Type	Lossy compression	Lossless compression
Formats	JPG, MP3, WMV, MPG	PDF, GIF, PNG, MOV, ZIP
Examples		
Advantages	Smallest file sizes, least transmission time, reduces Internet traffic and collisions	Original quality is preserved / no information or data is lost
Disadvantages	Detail is permanently lost	Less significant reduction in file size
Example uses	Music streaming, online images and video, image libraries on devices or in the cloud	Text documents, electronic books, high resolution print documents

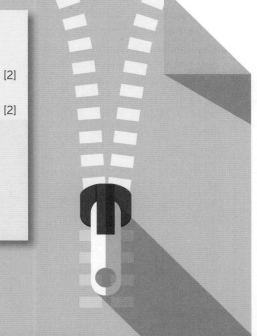

A large software program is being distributed via an online download.

(a) Give **two** advantages of using compression software for online downloads. [2]

(b) Explain which type of compression should be used to compress the software. [2]

(a) Smaller size on the server[1], reduces download time because it is a smaller file[1], reduces Internet traffic[1], uses less download data for users on a limited tariff[1].

(b) Lossless compression[1] software must be used as no data in the software program can be lost[1].
Lost data would prevent the software from running once uncompressed[1].

EXAMINATION PRACTICE

1. Construct an expression to show how many bytes there are in a 4.5 KiB text document. [1]

2. The ASCII character 'F' is represented in binary as 100 0110.
    State the binary value for the character 'C'. [2]

3. A digital thermometer is used to measure the temperature inside a warehouse.
    (a) The temperature value will be displayed to the nearest whole number using one byte. The historic minimum and maximum temperature values in the area have been −14°C and 42°C.
        (i) State whether a signed or unsigned integer should be used. [1]
        (ii) Explain why eight bits provides sufficient storage space for this value. [2]
    (b) State which of the values A, B, C or D represents the temperature value −6 in two's complement binary. [1]
        A. 0000 0110
        B. 1000 0110
        C. 1111 1001
        D. 1111 1010

4. (a) (i) State the maximum positive binary number that can be held in an 8-bit two's complement number. [1]
        (ii) Convert this number to denary. [1]
    (b) Convert the two's complement binary numbers 0011 1010 and 0101 1010 to denary. [2]
    (c) Add the two's complement binary numbers 0011 1010 and 0101 1010. [1]
    (d) Explain the result. [2]
    (e) Convert the two's complement binary number 1111 0011 to denary. [1]

5. (a) Convert the 8-bit binary number 0000 1001 into denary. [1]
    (b) Perform a right arithmetic shift of one place on the binary number in part (a) and convert the result to denary. Explain the result. [2]
    (c) Perform a right arithmetic shift of 3 places on the two's complement binary number 1000 1010. State the result in binary. [1]
    (d) Explain the result a performing a left arithmetic shift of 2 places on the two's complement binary number 1100 0001. [2]

6. (a) State the binary result after a right logical shift of four places on the bit pattern 0101 1011. [1]
    (b) State the result after a left logical shift of four places on the resulting pattern. [1]
    (c) Explain the result of these two consecutive shifts. [1]

7. A bitmap image with a colour depth of 1 bit has been created.

   (a) Convert the following binary data into an image with a resolution of 5 × 5 pixels, where 0 represents black and 1 represents white: 00100 10101 10001 00000 10101 [3]

   (b) Describe an appropriate compression method for an image designed for use on a website. [4]
   Full colour images are represented using 8 bits for each of the red, green and blue values that make up every colour.

   (c) Construct an expression to calculate the file size of the image above in bytes if the colour depth is increased to 24 bits. You do not have to do the calculation. [1]

   (d) Using 24-bit colour, the colour purple can be represented by the hexadecimal code #902EA6.
   (i) Complete the conversion table below to find the green and blue values in binary. [2]

	Red		Green		Blue	
Hex	9	0	2	E	A	6
Binary	1001 0000					

   (ii) Explain why hexadecimal is commonly used to represent colour values. [2]

8. A sound recording is made of a short piece of music. The quality of the playback is poor.
   Two factors which may account for this are bit depth and amplitude.
   (a) Explain the difference between bit depth and amplitude. [2]
   (b) Explain how bit depth could affect the quality of a sound recording. [2]
   (c) Describe **one** factor besides bit depth which will affect the file size of a sound recording. [2]

SYSTEMS ARCHITECTURE

The purpose of the CPU

The purpose of the **Central Processing Unit** (**CPU**) is to continuously fetch, read and execute instructions stored in memory by repeatedly carrying out the **fetch-execute cycle**. The CPU contains the **Arithmetic Logic Unit** and the **Control Unit**, in addition to several general-purpose and special-purpose **registers**.

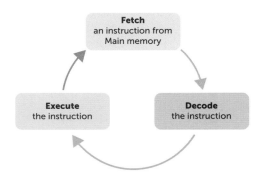

The fetch-execute cycle

Every CPU instruction is fetched from memory. Once fetched, it is decoded by the Control Unit to find out what to do with it. Then the instruction is executed. Every operation carried out within the fetch-execute cycle is regulated by a 'tick' or cycle of the CPU clock.

Fetch an instruction from Main memory

Decode the instruction

Execute the instruction

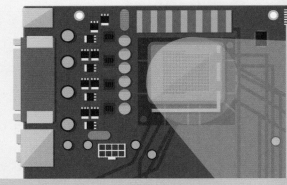

A single core 4.5 GHz processor has 4,500,000,000 clock cycles or 'ticks' a second. This is known as the clock speed.

Von Neumann architecture

John von Neumann developed the **stored program computer**. In a von Neumann computer, both programs and the data they use are stored in memory.

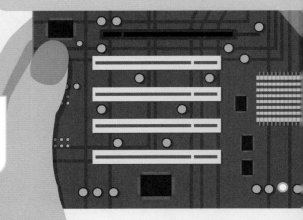

CPU component	Function
ALU (Arithmetic Logic Unit)	Carries out mathematical and logical operations including AND, OR and NOT, and binary shifts. It compares values held in registers.
CU (Control Unit)	Coordinates all of the CPU's actions in the fetch-decode-execute cycle and decodes instructions. Sends and receives control signals to fetch and write data.
Clock	The clock regulates the speed and timing of all signals and computer functions.
Registers	Very small, very fast memory locations. Registers are built into the CPU chip to temporarily store memory addresses, instructions or data. They are used in the fetch-execute cycle for specific purposes.
Address, data and **control buses**	Wires used to transfer data, instructions, memory addresses (of data and instructions), and control signals from one component to another.

Clock speed

The **clock speed** determines the number of **fetch-execute cycles** per second. Every action taking place in the CPU takes place on a tick of the clock, or clock cycle. Each cycle is one **hertz** so a 3.7 GHz processor will cycle at 3.7 billion times per second.

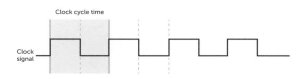

Clock cycle time

Clock signal

Identify **two** events that happen during the fetch-decode-execute cycle. [2]

The address of the next instruction to be executed is held in the PC.[1] The CPU fetches the instruction and data from memory[1] and stores them in its registers[1]. The PC is incremented[1]. The Control Unit decodes the instruction[1] and the instruction is executed[1].

MDR holds data or a program instruction when it is fetched from memory or data that is waiting to be written to memory.

The **accumulator** is a register in which results of operations carried out in the **ALU** are stored.

PC is a register which holds the **memory address** of the next instruction to be processed.

MAR holds the address (location in memory) of the current instruction or piece of data to be fetched or stored.

CPU

Data bus

Memory Data Register ⟷ Accumulator

Arithmetic Logic Unit

Program Counter

Control bus

Main Memory

Control Unit

Current Instruction Register → Memory Address Register

Address bus

3.1.1

MAIN MEMORY

Main memory (RAM or ROM) is directly accessible by the CPU. It is also known as primary storage.

The need for primary storage

RAM (**Random Access Memory**) is required to temporarily store the programs, instructions and data the computer needs whilst it is in operation. These are copied from the hard disk into main memory when they are required because it would be too slow to access everything directly from the hard disk.

RAM and ROM

RAM is the computer's temporary working memory. It is **volatile** which means it gets wiped as soon as the power is switched off. **ROM** (**Read Only Memory**) stores instructions and data that never need to be changed, such as the computer's start-up instructions so that it knows what to do when you push the 'on' button. ROM is **non-volatile**. As it is read-only, you cannot overwrite its contents once it has been set by the manufacturer.

Abeel had a power cut whilst working on a spreadsheet document. He said that he lost the entire document but could still open the spreadsheet program when the power came back on.

Explain why this was the case for Abeel. [2]

The spreadsheet program was stored on the hard drive and copied to RAM / main memory while the program was in use.[1] The document was created and stored in RAM[1], and disappeared because it was never saved.[1] If the document had been saved, it would have been copied to the hard disk.[1]

3.1.3

EMBEDDED SYSTEMS

An **embedded system** is used to control the function of electronic devices such as those commonly found in the home. They often don't need a full operating system since they perform limited and very specific tasks with their input frequently controlled by a button press or switch.

Embedded systems must be reliable since they cannot be modified once manufactured. The program that controls them is held in **Read Only Memory** (**ROM**).

Examples include air conditioning or heating systems, radio alarm clocks, washing machines, fridges, microwave ovens and digital cameras.

Jonny says that his car's satnav is an embedded system. State whether he is correct and explain your answer. [3]

Yes, he is correct.[1] It has one dedicated function[1] with simple controls. The user cannot change the software held in ROM within the embedded system. [1] The user cannot run other general software on it.[1]

SECONDARY STORAGE

The need for secondary storage

Secondary storage includes **hard disks** (internal and external), **USB flash drives**, **CDs** and other portable storage devices. We need secondary storage for longer term storage of files and data because it is non-volatile, which means your data will not disappear when the power is turned off. External devices are portable and may have very large capacities.

The advantages and disadvantages of different storage devices

	Optical	Magnetic (HDD)	Solid state (SSD)
Capacity	From 650 MB (CD) to 50 GB (Blu-ray Dual layer)	Up to 16 TB	Up to 4 TB for an SSD, or 256 GB for a USB flash drive
Speed	Up to 50 MB/s. Limited as there are moving parts	Up to 200 MB/s. Moving parts means relatively slow speed compared to SSD	Up to 3.5 GB/s for an SSD as there are no moving parts
Portability	Highly portable and lightweight	Internal drives are not portable. External drives are similar in size to a large smartphone	Flash drives and memory cards are highly portable. Internal SSDs are not intended to be portable but are very lightweight for use in laptops and tablet computers
Durability	Susceptible to scratches and will degrade over time and with exposure to sunlight	Good when not in use. Can be affected by magnetic fields and heat	Extremely durable
Reliability	Good in the medium term	Very reliable	Extremely reliable
Cost	50 GB for 45p	8 TB for £120	4 TB for £400

Construct an expression to show that one 2 TiB solid state disk can store the same volume of data as eight 256 GiB USB keys. [2]

$8 \times 256 \text{ GiB} = 2048 \text{ GiB}^{[1]}$ $= 2 \times 1024 \text{ GiB}$

$= 2 \text{ TiB}^{[1]}$

DEVICE OPERATION

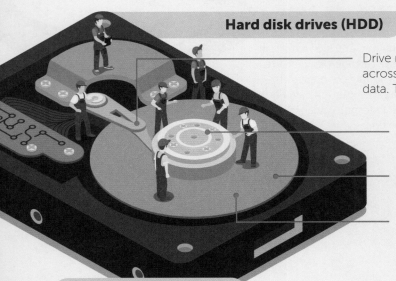

Hard disk drives (HDD)

Drive read/write head moves into position across concentric tracks which hold the data. This movement takes time.

Drive spindle rotates disk. Moving parts cause issues if dropped.

Magnetic platter stores data. Affected by heat and magnetic fields.

Iron particles on the disk are magnetised to be either north or south, representing 0 or 1.

Solid state disks (SSD)

SSDs look like a standard circuit board.
They use electrical circuits to persistently store data. These use microscopic transistors to control the flow of current. One that allows current to flow is a 1. Where current is blocked, a 0 is represented.

Optical drives (CD / Blu-ray)

An optical drive uses a laser to reflect light off the surface of the disk. One long spiral track contains pits and lands. When the laser beam hits the curved start or end of a pit, the light is refracted and a 1 is recorded. Where light is reflected back directly from the flat bottom of a **pit**, or from an area of the track with no pit (a **land**) a 0 is recorded.

Land
Pit   Pit

1000100000001000

1. Explain why hard disk drives have been largely replaced by solid state drives in portable devices. [4]

Hard disk drives have lots of moving parts[1] which can cause problems if dropped or shaken[1]. The read/write head moves across the disk and can scratch the disk irreparably if accidentally moved too violently whilst in operation.[1] Moving the head across the disk to read or write data reduces the access speed[1] that can be achieved with solid state devices that have no moving parts. The cost and capacity of solid-state storage is improving.[1]

2. Explain why secondary storage is necessary in most smartphones. [2]

3. Explain why a solid state drive is commonly chosen for smartphone storage. [4]

> 2. *Secondary storage is non-volatile.[1] Without secondary storage, you are not able to store photos, video and files for another session once the power has been switched off.[1]*
>
> 3. *Solid state storage is durable with no moving parts[1], so it will be more robust if dropped[1]. It is reliable which will mean few repairs or inconvenient faults.[1] It is portable and lightweight and takes up little physical space[1], reducing the physical size of the device[1], ease of use[1] and weight[1] of the phone for the user. Solid state storage has very efficient power consumption[1] providing longer battery life for mobile devices[1].*

Applications of storage media

Solid state drives (**SSDs**) require very little power and create little heat owing to the lack of moving parts. This makes them suitable for laptop and tablet devices commonly used on the go. The lack of moving parts also means they are very small and reliable – perfect for small portable devices with built-in storage such as cameras and smartphones. SSDs are also used in desktop and larger computers and are replacing hard disks in mass storage facilities as they can be 100 times faster and do not require expensive cooling equipment.

Hard disk drives (**HDDs**) are commonly found in desktop computers, but SSDs are frequently used for some applications such as the operating system and other software that needs to execute as fast as possible. **CDs** and **DVDs** are useful for archiving data in the short to medium term given a life expectancy of 10–25 years. **USB flash drives** may be more effective for more regular backup of small files as they are more durable.

4. Justify a different storage device for each of the following applications.

   (a) A database server in a busy office. [3]

   (b) Event photographs sent by post to a company from a photographer. [3]

   (c) Regular transfer of files between home and a place of work. [3]

> *(a) Hard disk drives (HDD)[1] have very high capacities[1] and are relatively inexpensive compared to SSDs[1]. Fast, durable and reliable.[1] (Or, could justify SSD on grounds of speed, capacity, reliability.)*
>
> *(b) CD or DVD.[1] Very inexpensive, costing only a few pence[1], easy to post[1], and will only be written to once[1].*
>
> *(c) USB flash drive.[1] Has sufficient capacity and speed for this purpose[1], very portable[1], durable[1], reliable[1] and inexpensive[1]. (Accept valid alternatives.)*

OPERATING SYSTEMS

System software programs are those that are needed to enable the computer to function, including the **operating system (OS)**, utilities, library routines and programming language translators. The operating system is a group of programs that is essential for managing the computer's resources.

Common examples of operating systems include Windows®, MacOS®, iOS® and Linux®. An Operating System (OS) has four major functions:

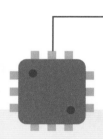

Process management:

The OS coordinates the CPU to **schedule processes**. All processes currently in memory waiting to be executed are held in a circular queue. The CPU allocates each process a **time slice** and switches to the next process very quickly, making it seem as though they run at the same time. Processes with higher priority are given longer time slices. This is known as multitasking. Each process has exclusive use of the CPU during its allocated time slice. Several time slices may be required to complete a process, so an unfinished process, now at the back of the queue once its time slice expires, awaits its next turn.

Peripheral management and drivers:

Peripheral devices connected externally to the CPU include printers, keyboards and monitors. Users must communicate with devices via the OS. "Out of paper" messages for example, must come via the OS. A buffer is used to compensate for the difference in speed between the CPU and the device.

File management:

The OS allows users to create, delete, move, save and copy files, or allocate them to folders. It can search for files, restore deleted files, free up space for new files and prevent conflicts when two users attempt to modify the same file at once. Access rights to individual files may also be managed.

User management:

Different users will each be provided with an account with their own user name and password. Each user can be granted different levels of access depending on their needs and levels of security. The OS can also monitor login activity and log out users after set periods of inactivity.

UTILITY SOFTWARE

Utility programs are small programs that are used in conjunction with the main operating system in order to manage extra features or functions. They are not essential to the running of a computer but make specific tasks easier or add an additional layer of housekeeping.

Four common examples of utility program are:

Defragmentation software

Files are stored on the hard disk in blocks. As different sized files are added and deleted over time, gaps appear which may not fit all of the next file to be stored. Files therefore become fragmented in order to fit them in. Eventually a good clean and tidy up is required that moves everything around to avoid fragmented files. A file saved in three fragments would take three times as long to find it all, so this process speeds up the computer's file retrieval and storage times.

Before disk is defragmented, it contains a lot of files, stored all over the disk

New file has to be saved in three different parts of the disk. Makes reading the file slower

After defragmenting, the disk looks like this:

New file can be saved in one place which speeds up read and write access

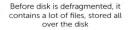
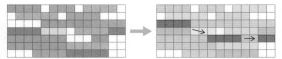
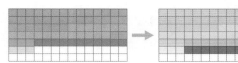

Data compression software

Compression software such as WinZip uses an algorithm to resave the data in an existing file using less space than the original. Sometimes data is lost (lossy compression) and in other times, the file can still be reconstructed without any loss of information (lossless compression).

File repair software

The data comprising a computer file can become **corrupted** if the disk develops a fault, or if a computer crashes during writing. Repair software can help recover the file.

Anti-malware software

Malware is software written with the specific intention of causing a nuisance or harm to programs or data. Anti-malware finds patterns of known malicious code in files and **quarantines** those files for deletion.

Compression software is a type of utility program.

    (a) Explain **one** situation in which compression software would be useful. [2]

    (b) Give **two** other examples of utility software. [2]

    (a) When emailing files[1], compression software enables larger files to fit within email attachment limits[1], it reduces the data transfer volumes to meet ISP limits[1] and saves space on a local disk[1]. Compression software also allows multiple original files to be saved as one single file[1] which is helpful for email and distribution[1].

    (b) Encryption software[1], defragmentation software[1], backup utilities[1], anti-virus or anti-spyware software[1], software firewalls[1], auto-update utilities[1], backup software[1], file repair functions[1] and disk formatting software[1].

IDENTIFYING VULNERABILITIES

Software needs to be written as robustly as possible in order to reduce the threat posed by misuse, malware, hackers and other attacks.

Robust software design considerations

Anticipating misuse is an important stage of development. A programmer should never underestimate the level of creativeness, laziness or malice of users of a new system. Every possible input, however incorrect or creative should be anticipated.

When **validation** or **verification** cannot resolve the issue, help messages and careful instruction should be used. **Authentication** is a process used to test that a person is who they claim to be.

Methods of authentication include a simple user ID and password, a PIN number or biometric methods such as fingerprint or facial recognition. These methods help to prevent unauthorised access to programs and data.

Audit trails

An **audit trail** provides a list of changes that have been made to software, by whom and on what date. They are sorted into chronological order so changes can be traced back to their original form to better understand any bugs or security flaws that reveal themselves for patching.

Code reviews

Code reviews involve checking your own program code with a colleague or partner to find errors that may have been left in it. This should happen after all initial checks.

Peer code reviews:

- Find vulnerabilities in the code that were not picked up in testing
- Streamline software development
- Improve the efficiency of the code and
- Improve programmers' skill levels by identifying poor practice.

PROGRAMMING LANGUAGES

High- and low-level programming languages

A **high-level language** has a **syntax** and structure similar to English that is designed to be understood by humans. High-level code must be **compiled** or **interpreted** into machine code before it can be run.

```
speed = distance/time
print(speed)
```

Python, Visual Basic and Java are examples of high-level languages. These are hardware independent, meaning they can be compiled for any system. The programmer can therefore concentrate on programming their algorithms rather than concerning themselves with the architecture of the computer.

Assembly language is a **low-level language** which is typically used to control specific hardware components. The machine code produced by the assembler will occupy less space in memory, and will execute faster, than the machine code produced from a compiled program.

Source code	Compiler	Object code
Written in a high-level language		(machine code)

Translators

There are two main types of **translator**: a **compiler** and an **interpreter**. These work in different ways, each having different advantages.

Compiler	Interpreter
Translates the whole program in one go to produce object code	Translates and executes one line at a time
A compiled program executes faster as it is already in machine code	Takes more time to execute as each instruction is translated before it is executed
Produces an executable file so the original code does not need to be compiled again	Original code will be interpreted or translated every time it is run
No need for the compiler to be present when the object code is run	The interpreter must be installed to run the program

Describe the need for a translator when using a high-level language. [2]

A translator (compiler or interpreter) converts high-level code into machine code or binary[1] to enable the code to be run[1].

EXAMINATION PRACTICE

1. Identify which **one** of the following defines the role of a register in a CPU. [1]
   A. It coordinates all of the CPU's actions throughout the fetch-execute cycle
   B. It temporarily stores data, addresses or the results of calculations
   C. It regulates the clock speed
   D. It holds the address of the next instruction to be performed

2. Two components within a modern CPU are the Control Unit (CU) and the Arithmetic Logic Unit (ALU).
   Describe the function of each.
   (a) Control Unit [2]
   (b) Arithmetic Logic Unit [2]

3. A tablet computer is being designed with 256 GiB storage.
   Suggest **one** suitable storage device. Justify your answer. [3]

4. Describe the function of an optical disk drive. [3]

5. Computer systems may either be described as 'embedded' or 'general-purpose'.
   (a) A fitness tracker device uses an embedded system. Explain what is meant by an 'embedded system'. [2]
   (b) A general-purpose machine requires an operating system. One of the roles of an operating system is to manage the users.
      (i) Give **one** other function of an operating system. [1]
      (ii) Describe how the operating system manages users. [2]

6. A computer is taking more time than usual to open and save files after a lot of heavy use.
   One possible reason is that the disk may have become **fragmented**.
   (a) Define what this means. [1]
   (b) Explain how a disk defragmentation utility can help to speed up the computer again if this is the case. [2]

7. PoundSoft is a software company selling accountancy software. Their software is compiled rather than interpreted.
   (a) Explain the difference between a compiler and an interpreter. [2]
   (b) Explain why PoundSoft sells the software in compiled form. [4]

8. A program for a new printer driver is being written in a low-level language.
   (a) Explain **one** advantage of using a low-level language for this purpose. [2]
   (b) Describe how a code review can be used to increase the robustness of the program code. [2]

NETWORKS

There are two main types of network: **LAN** (**Local Area Network**) and **WAN** (**Wide Area Network**).

A WAN connects LANs together to form larger networks. The Internet is the world's largest WAN.

The advantages of networking

Sharing resources

- Folders and files can be stored on a file server so they can be accessed by authorised users from any computer on the network.
- Peripheral devices such as printers and scanners can be shared.
- Internet connection can be shared.

Centralised management

- User profiles and security can all be managed centrally.
- Software can be distributed across the network rather than having to install it on each individual computer.
- All files can be backed up on a central server.

LAN

Operates on a single site or within a single organisation across buildings in a relatively small geographical area.

Uses Ethernet hardware and cabling that is usually owned and managed by the individual or organisation.

Examples include small company, school and home networks.

WAN

Used to transmit data over large distances, often nationally or internationally.

Uses third party or external hardware and cabling, including satellites, phone lines and the Internet.

Examples include the multi-national banking network and the Internet.

Describe **two** disadvantages of networking computers. [4]

If the file server is switched off or the connection to it is damaged[1], your files and folders cannot be accessed.[1] Faults may cause a loss of data.[1] Networks require constant administration and management to keep them running smoothly,[1] and the larger the network becomes, the more difficult it is to manage. This can require expensive maintenance and a skilled workforce.[1]

Other points which would score marks include: Performance may degrade as traffic increases.[1] Viruses can spread from one computer to another.[1] Additional security will be required to prevent hackers from accessing data.[1]

WIRED AND WIRELESS CONNECTIVITY

Data may be transmitted across a network using a wired or wireless connection.

Network performance is affected by the amount of data being transmitted across the network. In a LAN, if two or more devices are attempting to transmit at the same time along the same channel, data collisions occur, and the data has to be retransmitted. This is like two people talking on the telephone at the same time.

Data is transmitted through fibre optic cables using light signals, and through copper cables using electrical signals. Signal strength deteriorates with greater distance.

	Wired	Wireless
Transmission speed	Fast and consistent transmission speed.	Typically slower than cabled connections.
Range	Ethernet (copper) cable maintains a good strength up to 100m. Fibre optic cables can be up to 60 miles long.	Wireless hotspots are limited to a very small local area and require repeater devices to expand the range.
Latency Latency is the period of time taken for information to travel from source to destination. It can be observed as a delay in speech and video communication over very long distances.	Very low levels of delay in transmission.	Greater delay in transmission owing to additional error checking with the Wi-Fi protocol. The delay is particularly apparent when a live signal is transmitted via satellite.
Bandwidth The volume of data that can travel along a cable at one time.	Offers dedicated bandwidth between those computers at either end of the cable. Fibre optic cable can provide far greater bandwidth than copper cable.	Bandwidth can be shared by any users connected to the wireless network. This means it is generally lower bandwidth than a wired connection.
Interference	Copper cable can be susceptible to electrical or magnetic interference. Fibre optic cable avoids this.	Wireless signals can be reduced by walls and interference from other radio devices. This affects the connection speed.

Greater bandwidth allows more data to travel along a cable simultaneously. Imagine a motorway with either 4 or 8 lanes – cars (data packets) go no faster with more lanes, there are just more of them reaching their destination within the same time period.

THE INTERNET, IP ADDRESSES AND ROUTERS

The **Internet** is a global network of interconnected networks. The **World Wide Web** is the collection of web pages that are accessible via the Internet.

A network of **routers** passes data packets from one to the next until they reach their destination. An **IP address** is a unique public address for the outward-facing router or gateway of a network. Data **packets** use this address to travel to the router, after which point, they are directed using an internal (private) IP address within the network. For example:

IPv4 address: 212.58.244.66

Routers make connections between at least two networks. They read the source and destination IP addresses on each packet that they receive. Then they use a **routing table** to look up the next router on the way to their destination and forward each packet on its way using the most efficient path. Internal packets are kept within a network by not forwarding them.

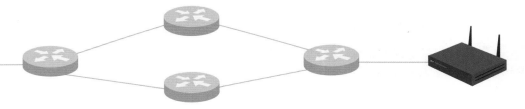

NETWORK SPEEDS

Data transmission speed is measured in bits per second (bps) or multiples such as kilobit, megabit or gigabit. A kilobit is 1,000 bits. A megabit is 1,000 kilobits. Speed is different from bandwidth.

The transmission time for a 35 GiB video file over a 60 Mbps connection could be calculated as follows:

Time = Size of file in bits ÷ Network speed in bits
Time = (35 * 1024 * 1024 * 1024 * 8) ÷ (60 * 1000 * 1000)
Time = 300,647,710,720 bits ÷ 60,000,000 bps = 5010.80 seconds (or 83.5 mins)

1. Write the following transmission speeds in order starting with the fastest. [2]

   A: 5G mobile data – 200 megabits per second (Mbps)

   B: Wi-Fi – 54 megabits per second (Mbps)

   C: Wired Ethernet – 1 gigabit per second (Gbps)

2. A live stream needs to download at a minimum of 120 megabytes per minute in order to playback continuously. Calculate the minimum connection speed required for this to work. [2]

   1. C, A, B.[2]   2. 120 MB * 8 = 960 megabits[1] / 60 seconds[1] = 16 Mbps[1]

NETWORK PROTOCOLS

Data transmission and communications standards have been developed to ensure that all connected devices can communicate seamlessly with each other using the same set of rules. A **protocol** is a set of **rules**. A network protocol defines the standards for data transmission.

The Highway Code establishes the rules for drivers in the UK. Without a standard, traffic would crash far more often. Likewise, English is a standard protocol for communication in the UK. Without a common language, communication would be very difficult. Imagine giving driving directions while blindfolded to someone using another language!

Ethernet and Wi-Fi

Ethernet refers to a set of related protocols or rules commonly used across Local Area Networks to govern how data is sent and received. **Wi-Fi** (Wireless LAN) is another family of related protocols which uses radio waves to transmit data. As long as a device has a Wireless **Network Interface Card** (**NIC**), it can connect to a wireless network. Like Ethernet, Wi-Fi has its own set of rules to manage data transmission.

Different protocols are used for different purposes:

Protocol	Purpose	Key features
HTTP (Hypertext Transfer Protocol)	Used by a browser to access a webpage from a web server	Delivers web page data
HTTPS (Hypertext Transfer Protocol Secure)	As HTTP with encryption	Encrypts the data and uses a secure socket layer for greater protection
FTP (File Transfer Protocol)	Transmitting files between client and server computers	Used to upload and download files from a server
POP3 (Post Office Protocol v3)	Retrieving an email from an email server to your device	Deletes messages on the email server once they have been downloaded to a single device
IMAP (Internet Message Access Protocol)	Accessing email on a mail server via multiple devices	Maintains synchronisation of an email account across all devices
SMTP (Simple Mail Transfer Protocol)	Sending email messages between mail servers	Used for sending only

Customers can access their bank via an online banking website on portable tablet computers.

Once logged in, customers can access their account data.

(a) Give a suitable protocol that could be used to transmit the account data. [1]

(b) Give **one** reason for your choice of protocol. [1]

(c) The bank sends customers regular emails. Explain **two** protocols that are used in the sending and retrieval of email. [4]

(a) HTTPS[1], (b) HTTPS is a secure protocol that encrypts data in transmission.[1] (c) SMTP[1] is used to send the email to the bank's mail server.[1] This is passed to the client mail server.[1] POP or IMAP[1] is used to retrieve the email by the customer's email client.[1]

Bonjour   Hola   Salve   Olá

TCP/IP LAYERS

Transmission Control Protocol / Internet Protocol (TCP/IP) is a set of protocols operating on different layers. A **layer** provides a division of network functionality so that each layer can operate and be updated completely independently of any other layer.

The 4-layer TCP/IP model

The roles of each layer

The **application layer** selects the most appropriate **protocol** based on the application operating on that layer. For example, HTTP or HTTPS would be used if using a browser, or SMTP for email.

The **transport layer** establishes a connection with the recipient computer. It then splits the data into manageable chunks called **packets** and gives them a packet number, (e.g. Packet 1 of 40) before they are passed on to the Internet Layer. Any lost packets are resent. The transport layer also reassembles any packets received into the right order.

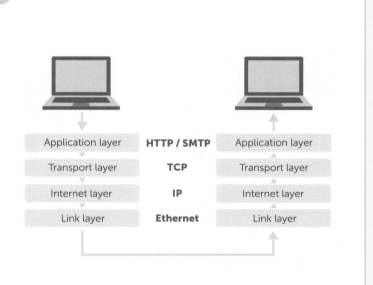

The **Internet layer** packages or unpackages data, adds the destination **IP address** and routes the packet to the next router on the way to its destination. Routers operate on the Internet layer.

The **link layer** is the physical hardware connection between network nodes. It uses the **MAC address** of Network Interface Cards to identify specific devices.

Describe **two** benefits of using protocol layers.   [4]

Layers are self-contained with their own separate purposes[1] so manufacturers of hardware and software that operate on one layer need only be concerned with that layer's protocols[1]. This makes it possible for hardware from one manufacturer designed specifically to work on one particular layer to work with hardware produced for another layer by another manufacturer.[1] Software developers are also able to edit one layer without affecting others.[1] Layers provide more manageable divisions of work than one larger system.[1]

TOPOLOGIES

There are three main networking structures or topologies to understand for this course. These are **bus**, **star** and **mesh** topologies.

Bus network

Bus networks can be used to connect computers in a small organisation. All signals are transmitted through a single backbone cable (or bus). There are terminators fitted to either end to prevent stray signals bouncing back down the cable.

Advantages
- Simple to install.
- A single cable significantly reduces cabling costs.

Disadvantages
- A cable failure in the main bus will affect the entire network.
- Performance of the network degrades quickly with more users. The data packets collide with each other as they travel in both directions on the same cable, and have to be retransmitted.
- Each computer attached to the cable can 'see' all data travelling up and down it which can be a security risk.

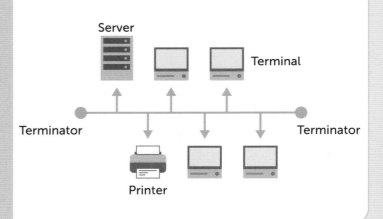

Describe **two** advantages and **two** disadvantages of the star topology. [8]

Advantages: Very reliable[1] as if one cable fails, the other nodes will be unaffected.[1] Data collisions can be avoided[1] by using this topology with a switch. This improves network performance.[1]

Disadvantages: A cable is required to connect every computer[1] which can be expensive[1] and requires a switch to direct transmission to the correct networked device[1]. If the switch fails[1], all devices on the network will lose their network connection[1].

Exam tip: This question requires 4 points for 8 marks. Give two advantages and disadvantages and then give a reason why each point is valid. Using words such as 'because', 'so' and 'as' will help you justify each response.

Star networks

Star networks are most commonly used in businesses and organisations where performance and security is essential. They are also found in smaller offices and home networks owing to their simplicity. Each device on the network is connected to a central **switch** which directs transmissions to the correct device using its unique **MAC address**. Some home routers also have switch and wireless access point capabilities.

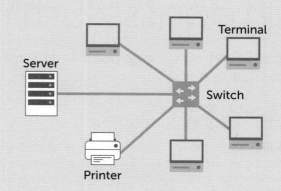

Mesh networks

Mesh networks can be used to connect small offices or entire cities. Wireless examples are most common, providing very large networks supporting traffic management and home automation systems. In a full mesh topology, every node is connected to every other node. Each node sends its own signals and in addition, relays data from other nodes.

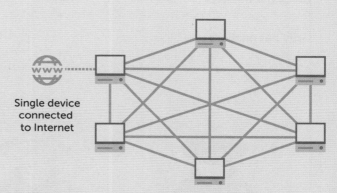

More common is the partial mesh topology, where some of the devices may be connected to only one or two others. This is less costly and reduces redundancy.

Advantages of mesh networks	Disadvantages of mesh networks
• Highly robust as the network will automatically find a different route if there is a fault with one connection or node. • Data can be transmitted from several devices simultaneously. The network can cope with high traffic. • Local networks run faster than in a star network because data does not have to travel via a central switch.	• The network is very expensive to set up as it is difficult to establish the connections. • Self-maintenance and network administration is complex; it may be difficult to expand the network.

NETWORK SECURITY

In the world of security, people are employed by companies to try and break into their systems.

Ethical hacking

White hat hackers operate within legal, ethical and moral boundaries. They are commonly employed by companies to deliberately find weaknesses in their systems and report these back to them so that they can be patched to improve the company's cyber security.

Black hat hackers are criminals who break into computer systems without authorisation. They are unethical, commonly have malicious intentions and are motivated by personal gain.

Grey hat hackers operate in between. They typically have no malicious intent but do not always obtain permission from the system owners before trying to find weaknesses. If a vulnerability is found, they will often let the organisation know and may offer to fix it for a fee.

Penetration testing

Penetration testing, or **pen testing**, is used to find weaknesses in a system by employing someone to break in. These vulnerabilities can then be fixed before a hacker has an opportunity to discover and exploit them.

Black-box pen testing

Black-box pen testing (External pen testing) aims to discover flaws and back doors into a system from outside the organisation – this might target servers and firewalls. This is done without the knowledge or use of usernames, passwords or access codes.

White-box pen testing

White-box pen testing (Internal pen testing) puts the tester in the position of an employee or malicious insider who may already have a degree of access into the system. Just how much damage could a dishonest employee cause?

Explain **one** advantage of white-box penetration testing over black-box testing. [2]

White box testing allows access with full transparency of the ways in which an organisation works, its infrastructure and its code.[1] This extends the testing area beyond where black-box testing can reach. This can find issues arising from a well-informed, 'inside job' by a disgruntled employee.[1]

METHODS OF PROTECTING NETWORKS

Networks require security measures to prevent unauthorised access. This ensures the privacy of data that is transferred within the network. Using a combination of methods provides greater protection against threats.

Using the correct settings and levels of permitted access

Access rights can be set up to allow different people different levels of use. Basic access rights can be configured as Read only, Read and write (or Edit), Execute (which allows a program to be run) and Full access which enables such a user to edit the rights of others.

Restrictions can be placed on access to drives, folders and files on an organisation's system. Ensuring these access levels are correct and not more than absolutely necessary for the job any individual is doing helps to narrow any risk.

Physical security

Locks on doors to server rooms and data centres provide a good level of physical defence. Other measures include **keypads**, card or **fob entry systems**, **fencing**, security guards and **barriers**.

Biometrics such as iris scanners, facial recognition and fingerprint readers authenticate your body measurements as your own. They may be used in combination with locks.

Give **two** security methods an organisation may use to protect data. [2]

Door entry locks[1], biometrics[1], security staff[1], CCTV[1], fire protection systems[1], passwords[1], secondary backup generators[1], off-site backups[1] two-factor authentication[1].

Firewall

A firewall is a software or hardware device that monitors all incoming and outgoing network traffic. Using a set of rules, it decides whether to block or allow specific data packets. By opening and closing ports, it can block traffic from disallowed connections from accessing the network, as well as blocking outgoing communications from the network, to make sure that only authorised traffic is permitted.

EXAMINATION PRACTICE

1. A business owner is exploring types of network prior to setting up a small office LAN.
   (a) Explain **two** differences between a Local Area Network and a Wide Area Network. [4]
   (b) Give **two** advantages of a LAN. [2]
   (c) State **two** advantages of a wired connection over a wireless connection. [2]
   (d) A router is installed as a component of the LAN. It has the IP address 192.168.0.1.
      (i) Explain the role of a router. [2]
      (ii) State the purpose of an IP address. [1]
      (iii) Draw lines between these devices to represent a star network. [2]

Server		Router / Switch

Computer	Computer	Printer

   The network's connection speed has been measured at 64 Mbps.
   (e) Construct an expression to show how much time a 4 GiB HD movie would take to download. You do not have to do the calculation. [2]
   (f) Other than speed, explain **one** other factor that may impact the performance of a network. [2]

2. A user enters the URL www.bbc.co.uk into their browser. A protocol is used by the browser to download the web page from the web server.
   (a) State what is meant by a **protocol** in the context of data transmission. [1]
   (b) State which protocol the web browser will use to download the web page information from the web server. [1]
   (c) Explain why a standard protocol is necessary. [2]
   Web traffic is passed up and down layers in the TCP/IP protocol stack.
   (d) (i) State which layer the browser would operate on. [1]
      (ii) Explain the purpose of the **Transport layer**. [3]

3. A network manager is carrying out a penetration test.
   (a) Explain the purpose of penetration testing. [2]
   (b) Describe the principles of how an internal penetration test is carried out. [3]
   (c) Explain how a firewall is used to prevent unauthorised access to a network. [2]

ENVIRONMENTAL ISSUES

Energy consumption of digital devices

The use of computer systems and devices consumes a huge amount of **electricity**. Many servers and devices are left on **24/7**.

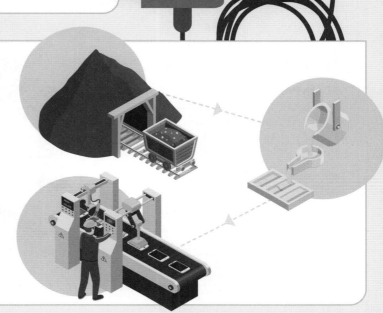

Manufacture

The manufacture of computers and electronic devices commonly requires **rare earth metals**, **toxic chemicals** and **oil-based plastics**. **Mining**, **extraction** and **processing** of these materials requires huge amounts of **water** and **energy**, can scar the landscape and creates harmful **waste** materials. Components are sourced from all over the world, including countries where **health and safety** and **environmental protection standards** are not always as high as those in the UK.

A legal firm replaces all of its computers on a three-year cycle.

Explain **one** advantage to the firm and **one** disadvantage to the firm of doing this. [4]

Advantages: Computers will be newer and probably faster and more energy efficient[1]. This increases productivity and lowers electricity costs[1]. Newer software cannot always run on older machines[1].

Disadvantages: Costs of replacing computer hardware may be high[1] (but less than the cost of low productivity or upgrading hardware). The firm is obliged to dispose of the e-waste properly which may have a cost associated with it[1].
Replacement may increase their carbon footprint[1].

Disposal of IT systems

Electronic waste (or **e-waste**) must be disposed of correctly in accordance with the **Waste Electrical and Equipment Regulations** (**WEEE**) 2019, designed to ensure that less harmful electrical waste is sent to landfill. Some nations accept e-waste for processing in their own countries, but this can often end up in waste heaps, leaching poisonous substances into the environment.

In 2019, there were an estimated 2 billion computers in use across the world including desktops, laptops and servers. There are a further 4.7 billion mobile phones — each of which may have been designed to fail after a given period. These will require manufacture, regular charging and careful disposal or recycling.

LEGISLATION

There are four main areas of **legislation** that need to be understood:

- The Data Protection Act 2018
- Computer Misuse Act 1990
- Copyright, Designs and Patents Act 1988
- Software licences (i.e. open source and proprietary)

Data Protection Act 2018

The **Data Protection Act** was updated in 2018 to incorporate the General Data Protection Regulations (GDPR). It has six principles that govern how data should be stored and processed.

These state that data must be:

1. Fairly and lawfully processed
2. Used for specific purposes only
3. Adequate, relevant and not excessive
4. Accurate and up-to-date
5. Not be kept longer than necessary
6. Kept secure

In addition, the data must be kept in accordance with the rights of data subjects.

Computer Misuse Act 1990

The **Computer Misuse Act** was introduced in 1990 to make unauthorised access to programs or data (hacking) and cybercrime illegal. The act recognises three offences:

1. Unauthorised access to computer material.
2. Unauthorised access with intent to commit or facilitate a crime.
3. Unauthorised modification of computer material. It is also illegal to make, supply or obtain anything which can be used in computer misuse offences, including the production and distribution of malware.

For each of the following offences, state which section of the Computer Misuse Act 1990 would apply.

(a) Theft and resale of customer data from an organisation's computer. [1]

(b) Correctly guessing the password of a manager's office account. [1]

(c) Rewriting software programs to remove activation keys. [1]

(a) Section 2 [1]. (b) Section 1 [1]. (c) Section 3 [1].

Privacy, ownership and consent

Data collection is subject to the Data Protection Act to protect the privacy of data subjects. Organisations can be required to obtain consent to collect and store personal data from the individuals concerned. A complete data set of personal information may belong to the organisation who gathered it, but individuals have a right to their own data. It is often unclear who owns data.

ETHICAL ISSUES

AI and machine learning

Artificial intelligence refers to computer systems that are able to act in ways that appear intelligent. Using **machine learning**, computers can use large data sets to train themselves how to respond in a huge number of circumstances.

DAILY NEWS
Word · Business · Finance · Lifestyle · Travel · Sport · Weather
2020   № 7674177203

Oil and gas companies denied Google's AI tools
May 2020

In an effort to reduce global carbon emissions, Google has pledged to stop supplying AI tools that can aid the discovery of fossil fuels around the world.

WORLD NEWS
Word · Business · Finance · Lifestyle · Travel · Sport · Weather
Since 1914   № 76834559

Major tech firms restrict police access to facial recognition software
June 2020

Microsoft, IBM and Amazon have withdrawn access to its AI software until a national law is in place to govern its use. This comes amid concern that recognition software may violate civil and human rights until it can represent everyone without bias.

Smart speakers

Smart speakers and **personal digital assistants** in smartphones with built in home assistant technologies have grown in popularity in recent years. They use machine-learning technology to better predict our requests and questions based on data collected from our previous interactions and those of people deemed 'similar' to us.

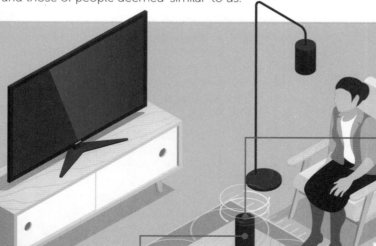

Algorithmic bias
"You may also like...."
We may be associated with things or people we would rather not be, based on our questions and the connections made by a computer. This might negatively influence its output.

Accountability
"Message sent."
Who is accountable if the device sends something insulting to the wrong person or provides misguided advice? The owner, the programmer or the manufacturer?

Ethical issues
"I love Marvin."
The data it collects, listening to private conversations in the home, may no longer be private. Data may be analysed and shared with other organisations.

ROBOTICS

Artificial intelligence and/or robots are increasingly being tested and used in healthcare, legal decisions, media content filtering and self-driving vehicles. Like most new technologies, they come with several factors that should be carefully considered before introduction into society.

Self-driving vehicles

Safety and algorithmic bias include factors such as how the car should be programmed to respond to an object, animal, child or group of adults suddenly appearing in the road. Applying the brakes hard immediately shifts the risk from the obstacle to the passengers, but is this always the right decision? Eastern and western societies have differing views on who should be spared in such incidents if an accident is likely to harm at least one party inside or outside of the vehicle. Under normal circumstances, the driver is responsible for such decisions.

Legal liability and accountability: In the event of an accident and ensuing legal cases, who takes the blame? The programmer, the manufacturer, the driver or someone else? What if the driver has a setting for a driving preference which increases risk for some while reducing it for others?

Robots and AI in healthcare

Robots and AI are used in dozens of ways in hospitals. For example:

- AI software can suggest a diagnosis when patient symptoms are input
- Cardiac pacemakers can keep patients alive
- Robots assist in surgery, allowing doctors to conduct surgery through a tiny incision

As with many new technologies, there are ethical and legal issues to consider. What are doctors supposed to do in the event that a patient wants their pacemaker deactivated or removed? Could a hospital be sued if robot assisted surgery went wrong? Who is at fault if a pacemaker is hacked?

Driverless cars are currently being tested on public roads. Discuss the ethical and legal issues that should be considered when creating autonomous vehicles. [6]

Ethical issues include safer and more lawful driving, as there is no room for human error or poor judgement regarding traffic regulations.[1] Some machines may not be sophisticated enough to make the best judgements affecting lives, in all circumstances.[1] The responsibility for safe driving is largely transferred from the driver to the software manufacturer.[1] Pollution may lessen in some areas owing to zero emissions in autonomous (commonly electric) cars[1]. However, it may increase in other areas of the electricity and production supply chains[1].

Legal issues include liability in the event of an accident[1]. Cyber security of computerised vehicles[1] may cause legal problems - vehicle theft or software corruption may be possible through hacking[1]. Journey tracking, driver identification and the use of this data[1] may infringe personal privacy. This data would need to be protected by the Data Protection Act 2018.[1] Laws may need to adapt.[1]

Marks are indicative only. Refer to the band descriptions and levels of response guidance for extended response questions on page 94.

INTELLECTUAL PROPERTY PROTECTION

Intellectual property (IP) includes brands and inventions which can be protected by trademarks and patents, and items which are protected by copyright (e.g. books, music, video, games and software).

Intellectual property is one of the most valuable assets of most organisations. A long-running case between Apple and VirnetX threatens to disable Apple's Facetime and iMessage services after a jury found that the Apple software contained VirnetX's patented technology.

Registered trademarks	Patents	Copyright

Registered trademarks protect distinguishable brand logos, words and slogans. Examples include the Android symbol, the Facebook name and even Intel's "Intel inside" jingle.

An organisation can form a **licence** agreement to use a trademarked logo from another organisation.

Patents are granted by the government to protect inventions and ideas. Examples include smartphone camera design by Apple, wearable technologies and the RSA algorithm for public-key cryptography.

Until the patent has expired after 20 years, companies are prohibited from using these ideas in their own designs without a **licence** agreement.

Copyright is automatically granted on original software and written musical, dramatic or artistic works.

Permission to use a copyright work will be needed from the copyright holder. An acknowledgement or **attribution** of the original source may also be required.

FoldOut creates software for use with folding screen designs.

(a) Describe the likely impact it would have on their business if other software companies or individuals began to copy their software without permission, in their own, cheaper products. [2]

(b) Explain **two** ways in which FoldOut could protect their designs. [4]

(a) FoldOut might never recover the money they spent on researching and developing the design from sales[1] if sales are diverted to another company selling cheaper copies[1]. It might cause confusion in the market over who owns the designs[1], damage the FoldOut brand[1] or bankrupt them[1].

(b) Trademarks[1] on their logo or software name would enable FoldOut to licence their software to other companies, usually for a fee, while protecting their brand and trademark.[1] Patents[1] would provide exclusive rights to the designs for a period of time[1], protecting the innovative design and functionality to legally prevent others using them[1]. Copyright[1] would protect the designs of the screen layouts and branding from being used without permission[1].

SOFTWARE LICENSING

A **software licence** is a contract between the user and the developer or owner that grants permission to use software under given conditions. These conditions may stipulate a time period or further limitations such as non-commercial use only.

Open source software is licenced but free to use. The source code can be viewed and edited. Any derivatives of the work must also be made available (open) to others with the source code.

Proprietary software is created and sold by companies in the form of a licence. Users do not own the software or its copyright, only a licence to use it. They will not get access to the source code to modify the software and licences are commonly limited by the number of users. Microsoft Office® is one such example of proprietary software available off-the-shelf.

Freeware is free, but will require a licence, commonly restricting its use and distribution, much like proprietary software.

1. A piece of software is being developed to help university students with important timetable reminders.

   Developers are considering using either an open source or proprietary licence to distribute the software.

   (a) Discuss the advantages and disadvantages of each licence for the developer. [4]

   (b) The developers distributes their software under a proprietary licence. Several students make copies of the software purchased by another student. State which law has been broken. [1]

2. A utility company collects personal data about customers as well as their electricity usage data each month.

   (a) State which piece of legislation covers the security of personal data. [1]

   (b) Give **two** security measures the utility company should put in place in order to provide adequate security of customer data. [2]

1. (a) Under a proprietary licence, Damon is able to charge for his software[1] and his source code remains hidden[1] meaning that no one can edit or see how it works[1].

Damon may not wish to/be able to sell his software for much[1]. Therefore, he may consider a free, open source licence in order to help as many students as he can[1]. He will not get any income from the software[1], but it may help gain traction and reputation for his work[1] which would build a greater number of users[1], and he may be able to profit from advertising[1]. Other programmers may be able to improve his software too[1], but the open source approach may mean Damon loses overall control[1] over his source code and distribution[1].

(b) Copyright, Designs and Patents Act.[1]

2. (a) Data Protection Act.[1] (Data must be kept adequately secure.)

(b) Firewall[1], anti-virus software[1], passwords[1] or encryption[1].

MALICIOUS CODE (MALWARE)

Malware describes malicious software written to cause inconvenience or damage to programs or data.

Viruses and worms

A **virus** is malicious code that relies on a host file to spread itself.

A **worm** is a standalone program that can replicate itself.

They are installed on a computer without the user's knowledge or permission with the purpose of doing harm.

Trojan

A **Trojan**, named after the famous Ancient Greek story of the Trojan Horse, is a program which masquerades as having one legitimate purpose but actually has another. It is normally spread by email. The user is invited to click on a link for some everyday or interesting purpose, which then executes a program which may, for example, give the controller unauthorised access to that computer.

Ransomware

Ransomware holds a computer hostage by encrypting it until a ransom fee is paid to the attacker in control.

Keyloggers

Keylogger software hides on your computer recording your keystrokes and intercepting passwords to send back to a third-party cybercriminal for analysis. Keystrokes may also reveal email logins and company secrets.

Discuss methods that could be used to prevent or minimise the impact of malware infections on a company network.

[6]

Anti-malware software should be current and set to automatically screen new files[1] and regularly scan the hard disk or server.[1] Macro scripts in files should be blocked[1] as these commonly contain malicious code[1]. Regular backups will ensure that data can be restored if lost or damaged.[1] Backups should be regularly tested, stored off-site, and on a disk separate from the main network[1] so they are not affected by the same conditions as the current data[1]. Email links and attachments should be blocked or disabled.[1] Emails from unknown parties should not be opened.[1] Staff should be appropriately trained to recognise threats and the strategies to prevent them.[1] Pop-ups should be disabled using a pop-up blocker and the correct browser settings.[1] Software should not be downloaded unless authorised by a network administrator.[1] It should be up-to-date with the most recent patches.[1] A firewall or filter can be used to block access to certain devices or websites.[1] Employees should not be allowed to bring in removable media or use them on company computers.[1] Refer to the band descriptions for extended response questions on Page 94.

TECHNICAL VULNERABILITIES

Unpatched software

Operating systems, browser software and other applications software are continuously updated to improve their security. When vulnerabilities are discovered, software manufacturers correct the code through the use of a **software patch**. This can be downloaded, often automatically, and installed to patch any 'holes' or software bugs in the code.

Unpatched software leaves these holes open for misuse, especially since the release of a patch makes the security issues more publicly known about. Users are automatically notified of updates to software when they log on. These should always be installed. Using old versions of operating system software also leaves the computer vulnerable to malware.

Out-of-date anti-malware

Anti-malware software should be kept constantly up-to-date to ensure the most recent threats are detected. Commonly, the greatest threat from viruses and malware comes from those most recently released.

SOCIAL ENGINEERING

Social engineering uses manipulation to dishonestly persuade someone to divulge personal information by deception.

Phishing

Phishing emails redirect a user to a fake website where they trick the reader into divulging confidential information such as passwords that can be used fraudulently. Email and SMS messages are commonly used for this with fake offers of prize draw 'wins'.

Shouldering

Shouldering or **shoulder surfing** means to look over someone's shoulder when they enter a password or PIN.

Blagging

Blagging is the art of creating a fake scenario in which a victim may feel it is appropriate to divulge information they would not give out under ordinary circumstances.

Suggest **one** method to reduce the risks of shouldering when entering a PIN into an electronic Chip and PIN machine. [2]

Cover your hand when entering your PIN.[1] Ensure that nobody is directly behind you or within line of sight of your hand.[1] Stand close to the machine to obscure others' view.[1]

PROTECTING DIGITAL SYSTEMS AND DATA

A rigorous security policy and set of procedures will reduce, but may not eliminate, the threat of attack. **Hacking** is unauthorised access to programs or data.

Forms of attack and defence

Hacking
Brute-force attacks

Automated or manual attempts to gain unauthorised access to secure areas by trying all possible password or key combinations.

Strong passwords with limited attempts / Penetration testing 🛡

Hacking
Denial of service (DoS) attacks

Servers and devices are flooded with too many requests or packets, causing them to crash or become unusable.

Firewall 🛡

Botnet

Short for ro**bot net**work, a hacker will infect a zombie device which they can anonymously control to send spam, for DoS attacks or to mine crypto-currency.

Firewall / Up-to-date virus checker 🛡

Pharming

Cybercriminals install malicious code on your computer designed to redirect website traffic intended for one site, to a fake, official-looking website.

This can be used to harvest personal details from unsuspecting visitors.

Up-to-date virus checker 🛡

Hacking
Man-in-the-middle attack (MITM)

An attacker intercepts communication between the user and server to eavesdrop or alter information.

Encryption 🛡

Acceptable use policies

An Acceptable Use Policy (AUP) outlines how equipment, software systems, documents and knowledge should be treated by the members of an organisation.

It makes the expected behaviours clear so that everyone knows the boundaries of what they should do and what is not acceptable with regards to their daily duties and interactions with others.

An AUP will be issued to all new members of an organisation to read and sign by way of agreement. It will also outline the sanctions for breaching the agreement.

Did you sign an Acceptable Use Policy for the use of computer equipment at school? What is in the agreement?

Give **three** items that may appear in an Acceptable Use Policy. [3]

Appropriate use of equipment.[1] Appropriate use of the Internet and email.[1] Use of own password only.[1] Rules on strength and frequency of password change.[1] Restrictions on sharing of company information.[1] Communications boundaries with email and social media.[1] Rules on how not to behave.[1] Sanctions for breaking the rules.[1] How staff may be monitored by the organisation.[1]

BACKUP AND RECOVERY PROCEDURES

Well-laid response plans can dramatically improve the recovery times and minimise disruption for organisations hit by disaster.

Backup and recovery procedures

An organisation must consider how, how often and where to back up their data. Once backed up, they also need to have policies in place that outline what to do and how to recover their data should it become lost, stolen or damaged.

The backup process

Backups need to be scheduled to meet the needs of a business. Each **full backup** needs a large amount of storage. A business will often make a full backup at the start of the week, then just make an **incremental backup** of any new or updated files on the other days. This reduces the amount of storage required.

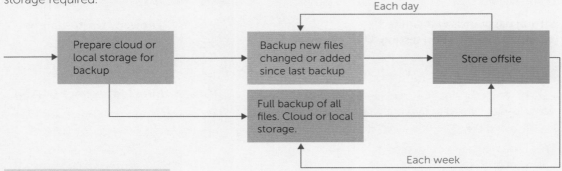

Disaster recovery plan

In the event of a disaster causing a loss of data, premises or essential staff, an organisation must have well laid plans to recover the data from a backup, with a schedule and timeline for getting back up and running again. In the event of a fire, plans should be made for emergency **alternative premises** or **home working**, and **alternative hardware suppliers** with the correct replacement stock available. The correct software will need to be reloaded onto each new computer.

Plans also need to be made to cover for **key personnel** who may become sick or unavailable, or leave the organisation at short notice.

AdSoft recently lost all of its sales data owing to accidental deletion.
Explain **one** way in which the risk of accidental deletion of data can be reduced. [2]

An onscreen alert could be used[1] to ask for confirmation that the files should be deleted[1]. Staff should be trained[1] to know that the deletion of the wrong files could have serious implications for the company[1]. Access levels[1] could prevent staff having access to the files in the first place, or limit the access to read only[1]. Backups of the data[1] can allow for it to be restored if accidental deletion has occurred.[1]

ENCRYPTION

Encryption is the process of encoding data so that it cannot be easily understood if it is discovered, stolen or intercepted.

An unencrypted message or dataset is known as **plaintext**. This is converted into **ciphertext** by encoding it using a mathematical encryption algorithm and key. Both the key and the algorithm are required to encode or decode data.

Simple encryption with a pre-shared key works like this:

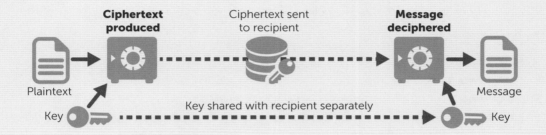

Caesar Cipher

A very primitive encryption algorithm was said to be invented by Julius Caesar. This is known as the Caesar cipher. This is a substitution cipher where each letter is replaced by another. The key in this instance would be 3 as A translates to D, three letters along the alphabet.

The Caesar cipher can shift forwards as well as backwards.

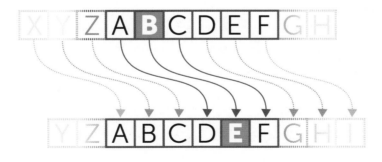

A student says that they have encrypted their work so that no one else can access it.

Explain why this isn't strictly true. [2]

Encryption encodes data making it unintelligible[1], but it could still be accessed and read, even if it would not make any sense to anyone who did not have the decryption key[1].

Using the same principle, decode the message "LSPH JMVI" using a key of 4.

EXAMINATION PRACTICE

1. Businesses commonly have a policy of replacing their computer hardware and equipment every three years.

   Discuss the environmental impacts of replacing working hardware and equipment so regularly.　　[6]

2. Computer programs are being used in some countries to help a judge determine the sentence when a person is convicted of a criminal offence. The algorithm is designed to accept input data such as the offender's criminal history, family history, social life, economic stability and opinions. It uses these to assess the risk of the person reoffending.

   Discuss the benefits, risks and ethical implications of using computer programs in this context.　　[6]

3. Part of an employment contract at a bank has an Acceptable Use Policy (AUP) which must be signed before anyone starts work.
   (a) Explain **two** items of behaviour that are likely to be included on the policy.　　[4]
   (b) Explain **two** reasons why company may wish to monitor staff activity.　　[4]

   The bank holds data on a database kept on the organisation's server about each of its account holders, including personal data, credit rating, credit limit and current balance.

   Social engineering techniques have been used by callers contacting their call centre.
   (c) Explain what is meant by social engineering.　　[2]
   (d) Give **one** possible consequence of such an attack on each of:
       (i) The bank's customers　　[1]
       (ii) The bank's staff　　[1]

4. A team is developing a new software app. They find some code online which has already been written to solve the same problem.
   (a) Discuss the ethical and legal implications of copying and reusing this code.　　[4]

   Once written, the team can release the software under a proprietary or open source licence.
   (b) Explain the differences between proprietary and open source licensing.　　[4]
   (c) Explain **one** advantage to the team of releasing the software under a free, open source licence.　　[2]

5. For each of the following state the most appropriate legislation applicable:
   (a) Unauthorised access and modification of company files.　　[1]
   (b) Failure to change customer details once informed they are inaccurate.　　[1]

TOPICS FOR PAPER 2
APPLICATION OF COMPUTATIONAL THINKING
(1CP2/02)

Information about Paper 2

Written exam: 1 hour and 30 minutes
75 marks
50% of GCSE

Specification coverage

Problem solving with programming

The content for this assessment will be drawn from Topic 6 of the specification.

Questions

This practical paper requires students to design, write, test and refine programs in order to solve problems.

Students will complete this assessment onscreen using their Integrated Development Environment (IDE) of choice.

They will be provided with:

- Coding files
- A hard copy of the question paper
- The Programming Language Subset (PLS) – as an insert in the question paper and in electronic format.

Students should then answer the questions onscreen using Python 3.

This assessment consists of six compulsory questions.

Python question files are held in the folder Python Exam downloadable from www.clearrevise.com.

Python solution files are held in the folder Python Exam downloadable from www.clearrevise.com.

DEVELOP CODE

Paper 2 is a practical programming exam. In order to do well in this paper, you need to be proficient in all the following skills:

- Be able to use decomposition and abstraction to analyse, understand and solve problems.
- Be able to read, write, analyse and refine programs written in a high-level programming language (Python in this course).
- Be able to convert algorithms (flowcharts, pseudocode) into programs.
- Be able to use techniques (layout, indentation, comments, meaningful identifiers, white space) to make programs easier to read, understand and maintain.
- Be able to identify, locate and correct program errors (logic, syntax, runtime).
- Be able to use logical reasoning and test data to evaluate a program's fitness for purpose and efficiency (number of compares, number of passes through a loop, use of memory).

The examples and questions in this section will make sure you are up to scratch in Python syntax and the techniques that you will need.

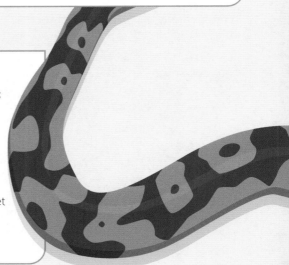

Python — A high-level language

A **high-level language** is one that is generally suited to the types of problem that you need to solve using computer programs.

The Python language subset

When you start learning to program in Python for this course, you will need a copy of the **Programming Language Subset (PLS)**.

This document specifies which parts of Python 3 you may need in the exam, and how the different Python statements are written. It may be issued to you by your teacher, or you may need to download it from the Edexcel GCSE Computer Science website.

You will be given a copy of the Programming Language Subset with your exam paper. You should use this as a reference to remind you how to write a particular statement with the correct syntax.

Make sure you are familiar with every part of the PLS document and are used to consulting it to check how to write a particular statement correctly.

VARIABLES, CONSTANTS, ASSIGNMENTS

Data used in a program is stored in memory locations while the program is running. A **variable** is a memory location holding a data item which may change value during program execution.

The table below shows the different data types found in programming languages such as Python or VB.

Data type	Type of data	Examples
Integer	A whole number	3, −170, 176500
Real/float	A number with a decimal point	3.142, 78.0, −0.5678
Character/char	A single character or symbol that can be typed	A, #, @, 6, !
String	Zero or more characters enclosed in quote marks	"yes", "Hi John"
Boolean	Can only take the value True or False	True, False

Some programming languages (but not Python) allow the use of **constants**. The value of a constant cannot change during the execution of the program.

```
const VAT = 0.2
```

A **variable name** can be a mixture of letters and numbers, but should start with a letter. Uppercase letters and lowercase letters may be used – note, for example, that the variable name `Total` is treated as different from `total`. The **value** of a variable (not its name) can change during program execution.

CamelCase is commonly used to separate words making up a variable name; for example, `totalCost`, `studentName`. Variable names by convention start with a lowercase letter, and constants are usually written in uppercase and 'snakecase' such as MAX_NUMBER_OF_PLAYERS.

Using a naming convention such as this helps to reduce errors in writing variable names in a program. If no convention has been used, it can be difficult to remember whether, for example, a total cost is named `totalCost`, `totalcost`, `Totalcost`, `total_cost` or something else. It also aids other programmers who may need to update a pre-existing program.

A **variable** is **assigned** a value in Python using the = sign.

```
costPrice = 15.65
count = count + 3          (This increases the value of the variable  count  by 3)
under12 = True
studentName = "Higgins, P"    (Python also allows the use of a single quote)
```

A game is being programmed.
(a) (i) Choose a meaningful variable name for the highest score in the game. [1]
    (ii) Set the highest score to 25. [1]
(b) (i) Choose a meaningful variable name for the name of a player. [1]
    (ii) Set the player's name to "Santos". [1]
(c) Explain the reason why variable names are commonly written using 'camelCase'. [2]
(a) e.g. (i) highScore[1] (ii) highScore = 25[1]   (b) (i) playerName[1] (ii) playerName = "Santos"[1]
(c) So they are consistent[1], easier to remember[1] and therefore reduce programming errors.[1]

INPUT / OUTPUT

When data needs to be input, the user is typically prompted to type something, and whatever they type is assigned to a variable.

The Python input statement shown below does this in a single line:

```
name = input("Please enter your name: ")
```

6.3.3

STRING CONVERSION OPERATIONS

Built-in functions are used to convert numbers into strings and vice versa.

Python function	Description	Example	Returns
float(x)	converts a string to a real (floating point) number	float("7.45")	7.45
int(x)	converts string to integer	int("356")	356
str(x)	converts a real number to a string value	str(67.0)	"67.0"
str(x)	converts integer to string	str(67)	"67"

Input

In Python, all input is accepted as a **string** data type. Therefore, if a number is being input, it must be converted to either an **integer** or **real (floating point)** number, whichever is appropriate.

```
visitors = int(input("Enter number of visitors: "))
roomLength = float(input("Enter room length in metres: "))
```

Output

The print statement is used to output data to the screen.

Example: Write Python code which asks the user to enter two integer numbers representing the length and width of a rectangle, then calculates and prints the area.

```
length = int(input("Enter length: "))
width = int(input("Enter width: "))
print("Area = ", length * width)
```

You can use the concatenation operator '+' instead of a comma ',' in a print statement, but you cannot mix strings and numbers. Numbers must first be converted to strings e.g:

```
area = length * breadth
print("Area = " + str(area))
```

PROGRAM-WRITING TECHNIQUES

There are several techniques that you can use to help make programs easier to read, understand and maintain.

Whenever you create a program, it is important to write it in such a way that you, or someone else, will be able to understand a month later what it is supposed to do.

- Use comments to say, for example, what the program and any subprograms are intended to do, who the author is and when the program was written.

- Use comments to explain any tricky bits of code.

- Use meaningful identifiers (i.e. variable names); for example, **totalMarks** rather than **totm** or even worse, **t**.

- Use white space (blank lines) between sections of code.

- Use indentation to show where loops and conditional statements begin and end. (Python forces you to do this.)

Rewrite the code below to make it easier to understand and maintain. Assume that the values entered represent a set of exam marks between 0 and 100.

```
x = 0
y = int(input())
n = 1
while x != -1:
    x = x + y
    n = n + 1
    y = int(input())
z = x / n
print(z)
```
[2]

```
#Find average of marks    [1 for comment]
total    [1 for meaningful variable names]   = 0
mark = int(input("Please enter first mark, -1 to end: "))    [1 for prompt]
numMarks = 1
    [1 for white space]
while mark != -1:
    total = total + mark    [1 for indentation]
    numMarks = numMarks + 1
    mark = int(input("Please enter next mark, -1 to end: "))

average = total / numMarks
print("Average mark: ", average)
```

ARITHMETIC AND RELATIONAL OPERATORS

6.5 **1.2.3**

Arithmetic operators	
Python	Meaning
+	Addition
−	Subtraction
*	Multiplication
/	Division
%	Modulus
//	Quotient
**	Exponentiation

Relational operators	
Python	Meaning
==	Equal to
!=	Not equal to
<	Less than
<=	Less than or equal to
>	Greater than
>=	Greater than or equal to

Modulus (% in Python) returns the remainder when one integer is divided by another. For example,

x = 22 % 5 will assign the value 2 to x

x = 15 % 5 will assign the value 0 to x

// in Python gives the quotient, so 17 // 5 assigns 3 to x, and 22 // 5 assigns 4 to x.

Sequence, selection and iteration

There are three basic control structures in all high-level imperative languages such as Python, C# or VB.NET. These are **sequence**, **selection** and **iteration**.

Sequence is simply two or more statements written and executed one after the other in sequence.

A **selection** statement comprises an **if** statement and a **relational operator** forming part of a **Boolean expression**. Variables of the **Boolean data type** can only be True or False. The logical operators **and**, **or** and **not** are used to combine two or more conditions.

Tip: A selection statement such as
`if flag == True:`

can alternatively be written as
`if flag:`

State what each of these Boolean conditions, written in Python, will evaluate to?

(a) `"Fred" != "fred"` [1]

(b) `1 <= 4 and 7 <= 7` [1]

(c) What will be output by the following statements?

```
a = 5
b = 2 * a
c = a + b
if (a == b) or (b <= c):
    print("True")
else:
    print("False")
```
[1]

(d) Write the condition statement
`if listSorted == False:`
in a shorter form. [1]

(a) True[1]

(b) True[1]

(c) True[1]

(d) `if not listSorted:`[1]

SELECTION

Selection statements include **if ...**, **if ... else** and **if ... elif ... else** statements.

The following Python code checks a user password:

```
password = input("Please enter password: ")

if password != "SP123":

    print("Invalid password")
```

1. Write Python statements to ask a user to input his or her age, and output "You are old enough to drive" or "You are not old enough to drive" depending on whether the age input is 17 or over. [3]

```
age = int(input("Please enter your age: "))[1]
if age >= 17:[1]
    print("You are old enough to drive")
else:
    print("You are not old enough to drive")[1]
```

Nested selection statements

An **IF** statement may be nested inside another **IF** statement. For example, suppose we wanted to output the largest of the three numbers entered. The Python code could be written:

```
if num1 >= num2 and num1 >= num3:
    print("maximum is ", num1)
else:
    if num2 >= num1 and num2 >= num3:
        print("maximum is ", num2)
    else:
        print("maximum is ", num3)
```

The elif clause in Python is a useful selection tool when there are several alternative paths depending on the value of a variable:

```
if member == "Junior":
    print("entry = 2.0")
elif member == "Senior":
    print("entry = 3.0")
elif member == "Special":
    print("entry = 0.0")
else:
    print("Member type must be Junior, Senior or Special.")
```

2. Write a Boolean condition to test whether **result** is between 1 and 10. [1]

```
if result >= 1 and result <= 10:[1]
```

*(**Tip:** Writing if result >= 1 and <= 10: is incorrect and will be flagged as a syntax error.)*

COUNT-CONTROLLED ITERATION

A **for** loop is a **definite count-controlled** loop. A count is automatically incremented each time the loop is performed.

This code will print all the numbers between 1 and 10:

```
for count in range(1,11):
    print(count)
```

Note that count goes from the first number in the range up to but not including the last number.

This code will print every fifth number from 20 up to but not including 100:

```
for n in range(20,100,5):
    print(count)
```

1. Complete the following Python program, which allows the user to enter a start number and an end number, and prints out all the numbers in between which are divisible by either 3 or 7, or both.

```
startNum = int(input("Enter start number: "))
endNum = int(input("Enter end number: "))
for count .........................
    if .............................
       .............................
```
[3]

```
startNum = int(input("Enter start number: "))
endNum = int(input("Enter end number: "))
for count in range(startNum, endNum + 1)[1]
    if (count % 3 == 0) or (count % 7 == 0):[1]
        print(count)[1]
```

Nested iteration

You can have one loop nested inside another.

Example: Display all the multiplication tables between 2 and 10.

```
for table in range(2,11):
    for n in range(1,11):
        answer = table * n
        print(table, " x ", n, " = ", answer)
```

2. There are two loops in the above code.
   (a) State whether they are count-controlled or condition-controlled loops. [1]
   (b) How many times will the print statement be executed? Explain your answer. [2]

   (a) A FOR loop is a count-controlled loop.[1]

   (b) The print statement is executed 90 times.[1] *The outer FOR loop is executed 9 times.*[1] *Each time the outer FOR loop is executed, the inner loop is executed 10 times.*[1]

CONDITION-CONTROLLED ITERATION

The **while** loop is a **condition-controlled** loop.

WHILE loop

A **while** loop is controlled by a Boolean condition which is checked **before** the loop is entered. In the Python program below, if **screenTime = -1** before entering the while loop, none of the statements in the loop will be executed. **days** will be 0 and the program will crash with an **execution error** when it reaches the last line.

```
totalScreenTime = 0
days = 0
screenTime = float(input("Enter first screentime: "))
while screenTime != -1:
    totalScreenTime = totalScreenTime + screenTime
    days = days + 1
    screenTime = float(input("Enter next screenTime: "))
print("Average screentime:", totalScreenTime/days)
```

Notice that the first screentime is entered **before** the while loop is entered. This ensures that the variable screentime is assigned a value before the loop is entered. All the statements within the while loop will be executed before the condition is tested again.

1. What will happen if the user enters -1 for the first screentime? [1]

2. Amend the above program. It should inform the user that they should enter a screentime of -1 when all the screentimes have been entered. Before calculating the average screentime, test that at least one screentime has been entered before the dummy mark -1. If no screentimes were entered, print a message instead of calculating and printing the average screentime.

   Add comments to your program and use white space to make it more readable. [4]

1. The program will crash because of a run-time error, division by 0.
2.

```
#Initialise variables and prompt user to enter the first screentime[1]
totalScreenTime = 0
days = 0
    screenTime = float(input("Enter first screentime or -1 to exit: "))[1]
    [1 for whitespace]

#Enter all the screentimes and accumulate total screentime
while screenTime != -1:
    totalScreenTime = totalScreenTime + screenTime
    days = days + 1
    screenTime = int(input("Enter next screentime or -1 to end: "))

#Test whether at least one screenTime was entered
if days == 0:[1]
    print("No screentimes entered")[1]
else:
    print("Average screentime:", totalScreenTime / days)
```

EXAMINATION PRACTICE

1. Load and execute the file **Exam Practice 6.1 Amend program error**, shown below:

```
total = 0
x = 0
while x != 100:
 total = total + x
 x = x + 3
 print("x =",x, "total =",total)
print("Total =",total)
```

Amend the program so that it works as intended. Save your program with a suitable name (e.g. **Answer 6.1 Qu1.py**) in a new folder. **You should save all the programs you amend.**   [2]

2. To determine whether a year is a Leap Year, with 29 days in February, the following rules are applied:
   - The year must be evenly divisible by 4 but...
   - if the year can also be evenly divided by 100, it is not a Leap Year,
     unless...
   - the year is also evenly divisible by 400, in which case it is a Leap Year.

   According to these rules, the years 1000, 1600 and 2000 are Leap Years, while 1800, 1900 and 2100 are not Leap Years.

   Load and complete the Python program **Exam Practice 6.2 Qu 2 Leap Year.py** to determine whether a year input by the user is a Leap Year. Save it with a different name in your own folder.

```
# Accept a year entered by the user
year = int(input("Enter Year: "))

# Check if this is a Leap Year
if year % 4 == 0 and  ............................
    print(year, "is a Leap Year")
elif year % 400 == 0:
    print(year, ............................)
..........
    print(year, "is not a Leap Year")
```
            [4]

3. The partially completed program **Exam Practice 6.2 Qu 3 Validate a user password.py** validates a user password.

   The user is permitted three attempts to enter the password correctly before being locked out.

   Complete the missing lines in the program **Exam Practice 6.2 Qu 3 Validate a user password.py**   [4]

   *You can find working programs in the folder **Python Exam Practice Finished Solutions**. There are sometimes alternative correct solutions which would score marks.*

DATA TYPES AND STRUCTURES

An **array** is a data structure used to hold several items of the same type.

For example, an array could contain the names of the days of the week. Python uses **lists** rather than arrays, but in many ways, they operate in a similar fashion.

In Python, a list is initialised like this:

```
day = ["Sun", "Mon", "Tues", "Wed", "Thurs", "Fri", "Sat"]
```

Items are referred to using their **index**, or position in the list, starting at 0. Thus the third item (Tues) in this list is referred to as **day[2]**.

A list filled with 100 zeros may be initialised with the statement: **day = [0] * 100**

Example: Write a program to enter the number of customers visiting a shop each day of the week and then print out the total number of customers for the week.

```
01  day = ["Sun", "Mon", "Tues", "Wed", "Thurs", "Fri", "Sat"]
02  customers = [0]*7    # or, customers = [0,0,0,0,0,0,0]
03  totalCustomers = 0
04  for n in range(7):
05      print(day[n] + ": ")
06      customers[n] = int(input("Enter number of customers: "))
07      totalCustomers = totalCustomers + customers[n]
08  for n in range(7):
09       print(day[n],customers[n])
10  print("Total customers",totalCustomers)
```

1. What will be output at line 05 the third time the FOR loop is executed? [1]
2. Define an array called numbers holding five numbers 37, 76, 55, 91, 23.

   Write code to reverse the order of the numbers, storing them in a second array called **reverseNumbers**. Print out the contents of **reverseNumbers**. [5]
3. Which variable in the example program above could have been identified as a constant by using an uppercase name? [1]

```
1. Tues: [1]
2. numbers = [37, 76, 55, 91, 23][1]
   reverseNumbers = [0,0,0,0,0][1]    #or, reverseNumbers = [0] * 5
   for index in range(5):[1]
       reverseNumbers[index] = numbers[4-index][1]
   print("Reverse numbers: ", reverseNumbers)[1]
3. day[1]
```

Note that there is no structured data type for a **record** in Python.

TWO-DIMENSIONAL ARRAYS / LISTS

An array may have two or more dimensions. A two-dimensional array or list named sales could hold the number of properties sold each quarter (Jan–March, April–June, July–September, October–December) by three different branches of an estate agent. An index number is used to reference an array value.

Index	0	1	2	3
Three branches **0**	56	87	92	43
1	167	206	387	54
2	22	61	52	14

The index for both row and column of the array/list starts at 0. In Python the list may be defined as:

```
sales = [[56,87,92,43],[167,206,387,54],[22,61,52,14]]
```

The number of properties sold in Quarter 4 by Branch 1 is held in `sales[0][3]` and has the value 43.

1. The three branches of the estate agency are known as Branch A, Branch B and Branch C.

   (a) Write code to output the sales figure for Branch C for the period April–June. [1]

   (b) What will be output? [1]

2. Write a program to ask a user to enter the name and five race times in seconds for each of 3 competitors, and display the average time for each competitor. [8]

1. (a) `print(sales[2][1])`[1]   (b) 61[1]

2.
```
name = ["","",""][1]
totalTime = [0,0,0][1]
averageTime = [0,0,0][1]
raceTime = [ [0,0,0,0,0],
             [0,0,0,0,0],
             [0,0,0,0,0] ][1]
for c in range(3):[1]
    name[c] = input("Enter competitor name: ")[1]
    for race in range(5):[1]
        raceTime[c][race] = float(input("Enter race time: "))[1]
        totalTime[c] = totalTime[c] + raceTime[c][race][1]
    averageTime[c] = round(totalTime[c] / 5, 2)[1]
    print("Average race Time for ",name[c], averageTime[c])[1]
```

LIST METHODS

Python has built-in list **methods** for creating an empty list, adding and deleting items. The ones you need to know about are listed in the Programming Language Subset.

The following program illustrates the use of each of these methods.

```python
#Section 6.3 list methods
#create an empty list
mylist = []
#or, you could write:  myList = list()

#append an item to the end of a list
mylist.append(7)
mylist.append("George")
print(mylist)

#insert an item just before an existing one at index 1
#the first item is at index 0
mylist.insert(1, "Dodgson")
print(mylist)

#delete the first item (which has index 0) in the list
del mylist[0]
print(mylist)

#create a list containing 10 zeros
listB = [0]*10
print("listB:",listB)
```

3. The above program prints five lines. The first line printed is:

   [7, 'George']

   Write the next three lines printed. [3]

   3. [7, 'Dodgson', 'George'][1]

      ['Dodgson', 'George'][1]

      listB: [0, 0, 0, 0, 0, 0, 0, 0, 0, 0][1]

STRING MANIPULATION

Concatenating and indexing strings

Concatenating means 'joining together'. So:

```
"Alan" + "Bates" evaluates to "AlanBates"
"2" + "3" evaluates to "23"
```

Each character in a string can be referenced by its **index**, starting at 0.

Thus, if `studentName = "Jumal"`

then `studentName[0]` will contain `"J"` and `studentName[3]` will contain `"a"`.

Other string functions that you may need are listed in the Edexcel Computer Science Programming Language Subset (PLS).

Substrings

Using indexing, you can isolate a single character or several characters in a string. For example, if the first three characters of a 9-character product code represent product type, and the next four characters represent the year of manufacture, you can isolate these strings using different **string methods** and string handling operations in Python:

```
productCode = "GAR201834"
productType = productCode[0:3]
year = productCode[3:7]
print("ProductType = ", productType)
print("Year = ", year)
```

This will print:

```
Product type = GAR
Year = 2018
```

Write a program which asks the user to enter a firstname and a surname, and outputs the surname followed by a space and the initial letter of the firstname. [4]

```
firstname = input("Enter firstname: ")[1]
surname = input("Enter surname: ")[1]
initial = firstname[0][1]
print(surname + " " + initial)[1]
```

String functions and methods

Example: **myString** is defined with the following assignment statement:

```
myString = "My name is Kenneth Lee"
```

To find the length of this string: `aLength = len(myString)`
This will assign 22 to **aLength**.

To find the starting index of the name "Kenneth": `pos = myString.find("Kenneth")`
This assigns 11 to **pos**. If the substring is not found, **pos** will evaluate to **−1**.

To find the first **n** characters of a string: `nChars = myString[0:n]`

To convert a character to its ASCII value: `aVal = ord("A")`
This will return 65 in **aVal**.

To convert an ASCII character code to a character: `myChar = chr(106)`
This will return "**b**" in **myChar**.

EXAMINATION PRACTICE

1. A list **name** holds the names of children named Anna, Dan, Peter, Sara, Vera, Zoe.

   An incomplete program is in the folder, named **Exam Practice 6.3 Qu 1 print list of names.py**.
   Complete the missing code. [3]

2. A list contains a number of scores recorded by someone playing a computer game. A program is to be written to do the following:
   - Define a list named **scores** which holds the numbers 35, 52, 19, 27, 68, 39, 53, 31
   - Sort the list into ascending order using the **sort()** method
   - Use a function to determine the length of the list
   - Delete the highest and lowest scores in the list
   - Calculate the average of the remaining scores
   - Print the result, rounded to one decimal place

   (Check: The correct answer is 39.5)

   Download the incomplete program file **Exam practice 6.3 Qu 2 List functions sort, len.py**.

   Complete the program. Use your copy of the Programming Language Subset (PLS) to look up list functions if you need to. [6]

3. A hockey team played 6 matches last year against each of five teams A, B, C, D and E.

   The number of wins, losses, and draws achieved in matches played against each team is recorded in a 2-dimensional list named **results** shown below.

	Wins	Draws	Losses
A	3	1	2
B	4	0	2
C	3	3	0
D	2	0	4
E	5	0	1

   The wins against team B are held in **results[1][0]**.

   An incomplete program is held in the file **Exam practice 6.3 Qu 3 wins, draws, losses.py**

   Complete the missing lines to print the element which holds the losses against team D.
   Calculate and print the total number of wins, draws and losses scored overall. [6]

4. A username is created by converting the firstname and surname to uppercase. Their date of birth is converted to the format ddmmyy. The three parts are then concatenated to form the username.

   For example, Colin Brady, born 17/01/2008 would have username COLINBRADY17012008.

   Download the incomplete program **Exam practice 6.3 Qu 4 string manipulation.py.**

   Complete the program code to assign a username to Jayden Carter, born 12/05/2009. [3]

TEXT FILES

Data which needs to be held permanently has to be held on a storage medium such as hard disk. The simplest type of file is a **text file**, consisting of a number of **records** each containing the same number of comma-separated **fields**.

Example

The text file **members.txt** was created in Notepad and is saved in the **Python in-text examples** folder, downloadable from **www.clearrevise.com**. This file is shown below:

```
001,Meadows,Jill,2018,S
002,Holland,Peter,2018,S
003,Henning,Gwyn,2018,J
004,Khan,Haroon,2019,J
005,Emerson,Jill,2020,S
006,Ganzoni,Luca,2020,S
```

Opening, reading and closing a text file

The following program opens and reads this text file, and splits each record into individual fields, using the separator "," specified in the split statement. Note that the last character in each record is the invisible newline character \n, which causes a move to a new line. Each print statement also causes a move to the next line, so your printout will be double-spaced.

```
#Sec 6.4.2 Read text file
#This program reads the text file members.txt
#splits into individual fields
#and prints all junior members and members who joined in 2020

memberFile = open("members.txt","r")
memberRec = memberFile.readline()

while memberRec != "":
    field = memberRec.split(",")
    ID = field[0]
    surname = field[1]
    firstname = field[2]
    dateJoined = field[3]
    memberType = field[4]

#the last field contains the invisible newline character \n
    if memberType == "J\n" or dateJoined == "2020":
        print(ID, surname, firstname, dateJoined, memberType)
    memberRec = memberFile.readline()
memberFile.close()
```

What will be printed by this program? [1]

Records for Henning, Khan, Emerson and Ganzoni[1], double-spaced.

WRITING TO A FILE

New records may be written to a file by opening it in either **write mode** or **append mode**.

Example

```
filmFile = open("films.txt","w")
```

This will create a new file named **filmFile.txt** in the same folder as the program. If the file already exists, it will be overwritten.

To add records to an existing file, open it in append mode "a". This will create a new file if none exists, or open an existing file after the last record.

The following program adds new records to the file newMembers.txt.

```
#Sec 6.4.2 Append records to an existing file
memberFile = open("newMembers.txt","a")  #"a" means "append"

newID = input("Enter ID, 'XXX' to end: ")
while newID != "XXX":
    surname = input("Enter surname: ")
    firstname = input("Enter firstname: ")
    year = input("Enter year joined: ")
    memberType = input("Enter S or J for member type: ")

#append this record to the file
    memberFile.write(newID + "," + surname + "," + firstname + ","
                        + year + "," + memberType + "\n")

#get the ID of the next member to be added
    newID = input("Enter ID, 'XXX' to end: ")
memberFile.close()
```

The PLS shows the syntax of all the statements you need to open read, write, append and close files.

`<fileid> = open(<filename>,"r")`	Open file for reading
`<aline> = <fileID>.readline()`	Return a line from the file. Returns an empty string on the end of the file
`<fileid>.write(<aString>)`	Writes a single string to a file
`<fileid>.close()`	Closes file

These are some of the relevant entries. Write Python statements to:
(a) Open a file named `cars.txt`, which has been assigned the fileID `vehicles`. [1]
(b) Assign the string "Renault, AU69HRW,2019,24698,\n" to a variable carRec. [1]
(c) Write the record to the end of the file. [1]

(a) vehicles = open("cars.txt","a")[1]
(b) carRec = "Renault, AU69HRW,2019,24698,\n"[1]
(c) vehicles.write(carRec)[1]

IMPLEMENTING VALIDATION

Data validation techniques are used to check the validity of data entered by the user.

> ### Example
>
> You should be able to write simple routines to validate input data. The following validation checks are examples of simple data validation:
>
> - **Length check:** a string entered by a user must be greater than or equal to a minimum length.
> - **Presence check:** a string should not be empty.
> - **Range check:** data must lie within a given range.
> - **Pattern check:** e.g. a postcode must conform to one of a number of set formats.

Note that validation can only check that the data entered is sensible and reasonable. It cannot check the accuracy of the data. For example, it can check that only S, M, L or XL is entered in a field for dress size, or check that a number between −5 and 35 is entered for a temperature in a country where the temperature is always within these limits.

---

1. A user is required to enter a 6-character ID in order to register on a website.
   Complete line 02 in the code below to ensure that a valid ID has been entered. [2]

   ```
   01 userID = input("Please enter a 6-character ID: ")
   02 while ...............................
   03     userID = input("ID must be 6 characters: please re-enter: ")
   04 print("UserID accepted")
   ```

2. A date of birth field has been validated.

   (a) Explain how the validated date of birth field may still be incorrect. [2]

   (b) Give **one** example of an invalid date of birth that should not be accepted. [1]

3. A validation check age ensures that the figure entered is between 11 and 18.

   (a) State what type of validation check is this. [1]

   (b) Write code to perform this validation. [4]

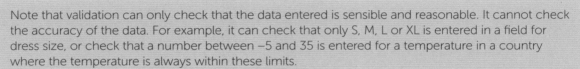

1. while len(userID)[1] != 6:[1]

2. (a) A user may enter a date of birth of 10/05/2005[1], but their actual birthday was 19/05/2005.[1] This would be accepted by the computer as a valid date of birth.

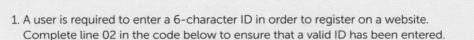

   (b) Any year or date in the future[1], any day greater than 31 or less than 1[1], any month greater than 12 or less than 1[1]. E.g. 32/01/2005 or 31/02/2005.

3. (a) This is a range check.[1]

   (b) age = int [1](input("Enter your current age in years (between 11 and 18: "[1]))
   while (age < 11) or (age > 18):[1]
   age = int(input("Age must be between 11 and 18 - please re-enter: "))[1]

AUTHENTICATION

Authentication routines

Authentication is a process used to test that a person is who they claim to be. Methods of authentication include a simple user ID and password, a PIN number or more complex biometric methods such as fingerprint or facial recognition. This helps to prevent unauthorised access.

Below is a simple authentication routine which checks that a password entered by the user is the same as the one held on file. (Assume this has been read into a variable named `validPassword`.)

```
password = input("Please enter password: ")
if password == validPassword:
    print("Password accepted")
else
    print("Invalid - Passwords don't match")
```

Looking up a valid ID and password

In a computer system which holds details of users or customers, typically each new user will initially be asked to enter a username and password which will be stored (in encrypted form) in a file or database.

When a user subsequently attempts to log onto the system, they will be asked to enter their username and password. The software searches the file (probably using a binary search) and if it is found, it checks the corresponding password. The user may be given three attempts to get their username and password correct before being refused entry.

The following partially completed program gives the user three attempts to enter a correct username. The binary search on the imported list is not shown here, but the complete program named **Sec 6.4.4 UserID authentication**, is in the program folder.

```
userList = [['BARL1240','password1'],
            ['BELC1168','password2'],
            ['CLAR5267','password3'], etc
            ]
found = False
attempts = 1
userID = input("Enter userID: ")

while attempts < 3 and not found:
    first = 0
    last = len(userList) -1
    #perform binary search on list (not shown)
    if found:
        print("UserID found")
    else:
        attempts = attempts + 1
        userID = input ("userID not found - please re-enter: ")
#three attempts to enter correct userID failed
if not found:
    print ("Invalid userID")
```

EXAMINATION PRACTICE

1. A program has been written to validate data entry of new stock items. Product code, size and price are entered, validated and appended to a text file "stockfile.txt".

   Carry out validation on product code, size and selling price.

   > Product code must be 6 digits long, e.g. 001256, 103333, 540000.
   >
   > Size must be S, M, L or XL.
   >
   > Selling price must be between £1.00 and £200.00

   Write the missing lines in the partially completed program **Exam Practice 6.4 Qu 1 validate and save stock items.py.**   [6]

2. A program asks a user to enter a password. The password must be between 8 and 16 characters, and contain at least one letter and one number. The password is appended to a list named "passlist". The list is printed out when data entry is completed.

   Write the missing lines in the partially completed program **Exam Practice 6.4 Qu 2 add valid password to list.py.**   [7]

3. A program has been partially written which:
   - Reads the text file members.txt
   - Splits each record into individual fields
   - Prints all junior members and members who joined in 2020

   The file contains the records in the format:

   ```
   001,Meadows,Jill,2018,S
   002,Holland,Peter,2018,S
   ```

   Complete the program named **Exam Practice 6.4 Qu 3 Read and print members file.py.**   [4]

OPERATORS

Arithmetic, relational and logical operators were covered in Section 6.2 on page 70. The questions on this page are designed to give you extra practice in using these.

1. A program has been written to record temperature readings of a patient every two hours over a six-hour period including the beginning and the end of the period. It records the number of times the temperature is 39 degrees or more, which is designed as in incidence of fever. Pulse is recorded and an alert is printed if temperature and pulse are both abnormal.

Complete the missing lines in the program. [5]

```
01 FEVERTEMP = 39
02 hour = 0
03 totalTemp = 0
04 fever = 0
05 while ................................
06     if ................................
07         temp = float(input("Input temperature: "))
08         if temp >= FEVERTEMP:
09             print("Hour:", hour, "High temperature")
10             fever = ...............................
11     if (hour % 3) == 0:
12             pulse = int(input("Input pulse: "))
13     if (pulse < 60...............................
14             print("Hour:", hour, "Abnormal pulse rate")
15     if pulse ................................
16             print("Hour:", hour,
17                     "Abnormal temperature and pulse: check patient")
18     hour = hour + 1
19 print("Incidences of fever: ", fever)
```

2. The formula for solving a quadratic equation $ax^2+bx+c=0$ is:

$$x = \frac{-b \pm \sqrt{(b^2 - 4ac)}}{2a}$$

Complete a Python program to ask the user to enter values for a, b and c, and solve the equation $ax^2+bx+c=0$. [3]

```
import math
a = int(input("Enter coefficient a: ")
b = int(input("Enter coefficient b: ")
c = int(input("Enter coefficient c: ")
if ................................
    print("Equation has no solution")
else:
    x1 = -b + math.sqrt(...............................
    x2 = ...............................
print(x1, x2)
```

1. Check the completed program *Sec 6.5 Check patient temperature.py*.

2. Check the completed program *Sec 6.5 Roots of a quadratic equation.py*.

SUBPROGRAMS

There are two types of subprogram, **functions** and **procedures**, which are defined and called slightly differently. Programming languages have many built-in functions, some of which you have already used. `input`, `int` and `len` are examples of functions you have used.

```
x = input("Enter a number ")  assigns the user input to variable x
num = int("345")  assigns the integer 345 to variable num.
stringLength = len("This is a string")  will return 16 in stringLength
```

Writing a function   6.6.2

A function is to be written that finds and returns the volume of a cuboid. The side lengths are passed as passed as parameters.

```
def cubeVolume(a,b,c):
    volume = a * b * c
    return volume
```

To call the function:

```
cubeVol = cubeVolume(2.4, 5.6, 7.25)
print("Volume of cube:  ",cubeVol)
```

Local and global variables   6.6.3

All variables have a **scope**, which defines the parts of a program in which they are recognised. In the function below, `totalScore`, `throw1` and `throw2` are **local variables**. They are not recognised outside the subroutine and if you try to print them in the main program, you will get an error message. The scope of a **global variable** is the whole program including all its subroutines.

Write a function throwDice to simulate throwing two 6-sided dice n times. On each throw, if the numbers on the two dice are equal, the score is twice the sum of the two throws. Otherwise the score is the sum of the two throws. Write a statements to call the function three times for each of two players and assign total scores for three throws to player1Score and player2Score.

(The Python library function randint(a,b) returns a random integer between a and b.)   [5]

```
import random[1]                          #import library module
def throwDice(n):[1]
    totalScore = 0[1]                     #totalScore is a local variable
#count is a local variable
#its scope is the for…next loop
    for count in range(n):[1]
        throw1 = random.randint(1,6)[1]   #throw1 is a local variable
        throw2 = random.randint(1,6)      #throw2 is a local variable
        score = throw1 + throw2[1]
        if (throw1 == throw2):[1]
            score = 2*score
    return score[1]
#main program
player1Score = throwDice(3)
player2Score = throwDice(3)
```

PROCEDURES

Procedures are similar to functions but are called simply by writing the name of the procedure. They do not usually return a value, and some languages do not have procedures. In Python, for example, all subprograms are functions.

Example

```
def greet(firstName):
    print("Hello ", firstName)
```

The procedure has one **parameter**, firstName. It is called by writing the procedure name, passing it the **argument** "Joanna" in brackets.

```
greet("Joanna")
```

This will print:

```
Hello Joanna
```

The example below defines a **global variable** called logo which can be used, changed or printed in the main program and in any of the procedures.

The procedure below displays a menu of options:

"1. Display rules ", "2. Start new game ", "3. Quit".

```
global logo
def menu():
    print(logo)
    print("1. Display rules ")
    print("2. Start new game ")
    print("3. Quit")

#main program
logo = "C O U N T   T H E   C H I C K E N S"

.........................  //call procedure
```

(a) Show how the subroutine is called. [1]

(b) How many parameters does the procedure have? [1]

(a) To call the procedure:

menu( )[1]

(b) This procedure has no parameters.[1]

EXAMINATION PRACTICE

1. A program has been written to test a user on multiplication tables. The program:
   - Prints a multiplication table for a chosen number between 2 and 12.
   - Asks the user which table they wish to be tested on.
   - Asks a question on that table, accepts the answer and tells the user whether it was correct or not.

   Complete the missing lines in program **Exam Practice 6.5,6.6 Qu 1 times tables.py**   [7]

2. A program and subprogram have been written to test whether a triangle is right-angled.

   The function **triangle( )** has 3 parameters a, b, c and returns True if $a^2 = b^2 + c^2$

   The user inputs values for the three sides and then calls the function.

   Open file **Exam practice 6.5,6.6 Qu 2 right angled triangle.py**

   Code statements to pass three integers **sideA**, **sideB** and **sideC** to the function.

   In the main program:
   - Enter values for the three sides.
   - Call the function **triangle( )**, passing it the three parameters.
   - Return True or False to the main program and print "Right-angled" if the function returns True, or "Not right-angled" if it returns False.   [7]

3. Write a program which:
   - Asks the user to enter a temperature in degrees Fahrenheit.
   - Calls a function which converts it to a temperature in degree Celsius, using the formula F = (C * 9/5) + 32.
   - Returns the result to the main program and prints it, rounded to 1 decimal place.
   - Repeats the above steps until the user enters a temperature of 999.

   The program should:
   - Include at least two useful comments.
   - Make use of another technique for making your program easy to read, understand and maintain.
   - Be tested with temperatures C = 0, −40, 17.1. (Expected results 32, −40, 212, 62.8.)

   Download and complete the program:
   Exam practice 6.5,6.6 Qu 3 Convert temperature C to F.py.   [6]

EXAMINATION PRACTICE ANSWERS

Topic 1

1. (a) It performs a linear search on the list for an item entered by the user. If the item is not found, it prints "invalid number". [2]
    (b) 13 (the number of items in the list). [1]
    (c) 4 times. [1]
    (d) As soon as the item is found, the print statement at line 08 is executed and the while loop is exited. If there was no flag, the linear search would continue searching the whole list even after the item was found. [2]

2. (a) It acts as a 'flag' which is set to False when a pass through the list is made and no items are swapped, meaning that the list is now sorted. [2]
    (b) temp = names[index]
         names[index] = names[index+1]
         names[index+1] = temp [3]
    (c) Adam Edna Charlie Jack Ken Maria Victor
         Adam Charlie Edna Jack Ken Maria Victor [2]
    (d) 3 passes. Swaps are made on the first two passes. The list will be sorted after the second pass, and on the third pass, no swaps are made, so swapMade is set to False and the while loop terminates. [2]

3. (a) [4]

num	a	b	ans
	0	0	
3	3	1	
8	11	2	
2	13	3	
5	18	4	
-1			4.5

    (b) It calculates the average of the numbers input by the user. [1]

4. [4]

A	B	C	D = A OR B	E = NOT (A OR B)	F = B AND C	X = E OR F
0	0	0	0	1	0	1
0	0	1	0	1	0	1
0	1	0	1	0	0	0
0	1	1	1	0	1	1
0	0	0	0	1	0	1
1	0	1	1	0	0	0
1	1	0	1	0	0	0
1	1	1	1	0	1	1

Topic 2

1. 4.5 × 1024 = 4,608 bytes. [1]

2. 'C' is three characters before 'F', so deduct 3 from the value for 'F'. 100 0011. [2]

3. (a) (i)   A signed integer would be most appropriate as this accommodates for negative values. [1]
         (ii) An 8-bit signed integer has minimum and maximum values of -128 to 127 which would be enough to store the highest and lowest recorded temperatures and more. [2]
    (b) D. 1111 1010 [1]

4. (a) (i) 0111 1111 [1]
   (ii) 127 [1]
   (b) 58 and 90. [2]
   (c) 1001 0100 [1]
   (d) Overflow has occurred, changing the sign bit. This gives an incorrect negative result. [2]
   (e) −13 [1]

5. (a) 9 [1]
   (b) 0000 0100 = 4 in denary. Each shift right divides by 2. Loss of precision occurs when the last digit dropped is odd. [2]
   (c) 0001 0001 [1]
   (d) 0000 0100. Overflow has occurred and the sign bit and value have both changed. [2]

6. (a) 0000 0101. [1]
   (b) 0101 0000. [1]
   (c) The leftmost bits of the original bit pattern are unchanged and the rightmost four bits are set to zero. [1]

7. (a) [3]

   (b) Lossy compression (JPG) would provide the smallest file size whilst maintaining a good quality image. Whilst some data is removed during the compression process, the image would still be recognisable. The smaller file size would mean it was able to download and display on a browser more quickly. Alternative compression methods such as PNG or GIF are acceptable with an explanation. [4]
   (c) 25 pixels × 24 bits / 8 = 75 bytes. [1]
   (d) (i) Green: 0010 1110, Blue: 1010 0110. [2]
      (ii) Hexadecimal is easier to remember than a string of binary values, so humans make fewer errors when writing it down or using it in code. Hexadecimal is a shortened notation of binary so uses fewer characters. [2]

8. (a) Bit depth means the number of bits allocated to each recorded sample. Amplitude is the height of a wave at a given moment. [2]
   (b) The greater the number of bits, the more accurately the wave height of each sample can be recorded. This increases the overall quality of the recording as it will create a closer representation of the original sound. [2]
   (c) Sample rate is the number of samples taken each second. As the sample rate is increased, the file size will increase as each sample is saved at the given bit depth/resolution. [2]

Topic 3

1. B – It temporarily stores data, addresses or the results of calculations. [1]

2. (a) The control unit controls the input and output of data and the flow of data within the computer. It coordinates all the operations of the CPU, using clock timing signals to synchronise the stages of the Fetch-Decode-Execute cycle. [2]
   (b) The ALU carries out arithmetic operations such as adding two numbers, and logical operations such as AND, OR and NOT. [2]

3. SSD (or HDD). SSD is lightweight and unaffected by knocks or bumps as it has no moving parts. It runs with less power so increases the battery life of the tablet. It produces less heat when running so a fan is not required, saving space and weight inside the tablet. If HDD is chosen, they have a high capacity and may be less expensive to install making the overall tablet better value. [3]
   (*Tip: Justification must match the answer you give. SSD is easier to justify here to gain 3 marks.*)

4. An optical disk shines a laser light onto the reflective surface of an optical disk. The disk has one long spiral track with pits burned/pressed into it. The laser light is reflected. When it hits the start or end of a pit, it is refracted, and a low light reflection is interpreted as a 1. A change in reflected light intensity determines the 1s and 0s that are read or recorded. [3]

5. (a) An embedded system has one dedicated function. It has simple controls and cannot run other general software on it. The user cannot edit the software running on it. [2]

(b) (i) File management, process management, peripheral management, memory management, security management and application management. [1]

(ii) Each user will be provided with a unique account and password. Each account will have differing levels of access to various files, folders or drives. Users can change passwords. Users may be automatically logged out after periods of inactivity for security. User activity can be logged. [2]

6. (a) A disk becomes fragmented when there is limited available contiguous space left to save a file in one space. Instead, the file must be split into smaller fragments with each fragment stored in the smaller, remaining spaces on the disk. [1]

(b) A defragmentation utility can help by moving all of the files around on the disk, putting each fragmented file back together again so that each file is stored in consecutive blocks. This makes searching for the file much faster as the computer needs only to move to one section of the hard disk rather than thrashing to many different locations. Saving a file is similar in that the computer can place a whole file in one area on the disk rather than lots of smaller fragments in different locations. [2]

7. (a) A compiler translates the whole program, producing object code which may be saved and run without the need to recompile. An interpreter translates and runs each line of code one by one. [2]

(b) PoundSoft sells the software in compiled form (object code) so that the purchaser does not need to have an appropriate interpreter installed on each of their computers. The compiled code is executable, unlike code which has to be interpreted every time before it can be run.
A second reason is that if they do not sell the source code, no one can view it or make changes to it.. This protects any clever algorithms they may have developed as no one can see how they work. [4]

8. (a) Low-level commands can execute more quickly than high-level code. Memory locations and specialist hardware can be referred to or controlled directly. The assembled program takes up less memory than a higher-level language equivalent. [2]

(b) Reviews by peers can help reduce errors by finding vulnerabilities not seen by others. Programmers can learn from each other's practices which increases code quality. Ways to make the code more efficient may be identified. [2]

Topic 4

1. (a) A LAN connects devices within one site or location; a WAN links more than one remote geographical location to another.
LANs are typically created using hardware and connections owned by a single person or organisation; WANs usually use a shared infrastructure under shared ownership / use third party connections such as phone lines and satellite connections. Data transmission speed is likely to be higher across a LAN than across a WAN. Encryption is more likely to be used with a WAN as it is more likely to be public. A LAN is more likely to be private and may not need encryption.
LAN connections can be more reliably managed as they are under local control by network administrators; WAN connections can suffer under heavy traffic, viruses or physical damage outside the control of local administrators or users. [4]

(b) Peripheral devices can be shared by multiple computers / users. Files and folders may be accessed from any machine or more easily shared. An Internet connection may be shared. User profiles can be managed centrally. Software updates can be distributed across the network from the server. Backup can be centralised. [2]

(c) Wired connections are generally faster, with a more consistent speed and greater bandwidth. Users may be unlikely to need to move computers around within the network area / computers will be in fixed positions. Walls may be very thick or there may be other devices that are likely to cause interference to a Wi-Fi network. Low / unnoticeable levels of latency.

(d) (i) A router receives and transmits data within a network. It is used to join networks together, such as a connection to the Internet. It uses a routing table to route packets towards their destination. [2]

(ii) An IP address uniquely identifies a computer or device within a network. [1]

(iii) [2]

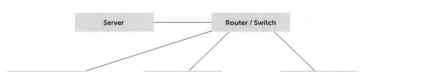

(e) $\dfrac{bits\ to\ transfer}{bits\ per\ second}$
e.g.: $\dfrac{4 \times 1024 \times 1024 \times 1024 \times 8}{64 \times 1000000}$
= 537 seconds = 8.9 minutes [2]

(f) Range – If devices are further than 100m apart, signal strength will start to deteriorate. Bandwidth – Copper cable will not have as high bandwidth as fibre optic cable so may affect streaming of very large video files. Latency – A delay caused by the transmission time between the sending and receiving of data. [2]

2. (a) A protocol is a common set of rules used to transmit data. [1]
    (b) Hypertext Transfer Protocol (HTTP); Hypertext Transfer Protocol Secure HTTPS. [1]
    (c) Without a protocol, there would be no way to ensure that every browser could access every web server using the same rules. The World Wide Web would fail to operate. [2]
    (d) (i) The Application layer. [1]
         (ii) The Transport layer establishes/sets up the connection between sending and recipient computers. It divides data into packets, sequentially numbers the packets and adds a port number. Then it reassembles packets into order once received, handles missing packet errors and resends replacement packets. [3]

3. (a) The purpose of penetration testing is to detect weaknesses in an organisation's computer security systems, so that they can be fixed. [2]
    (b) A "white hat" hacker is employed to put themselves in the position of a dishonest employee to see if they can find a weakness in the security system and gain entry to parts of the system and data which they are not authorised to view or change. Any weakness is then reported, and extra security measures put in place to fix the vulnerability. [3]
    (c) All incoming data packets are monitored. A set of rules is used to determine whether or not they are allowed to enter the network. Network ports can be opened or closed to allow or block data from disallowed connections. [2]

Topic 5

1. The volume of e-waste is increased. Working equipment is sometimes unnecessarily disposed of. It can also be illegally sent to landfill in the UK or sent abroad to be disposed of. This is a waste of resources, especially rare raw materials used in the latest technology that must be mined to be replaced. Mining causes significant environmental damage and some metals are already in short supply.
    Toxic chemicals are used in the manufacture of hardware and can leak into the environment if left in landfill. Some nations receive our e-waste and extract valuable metals through burning equipment which pollutes the air, waterways and the land. [6]
    This question should be marked against the band descriptions and levels of response guidance for extended response questions on page 94.

2. The benefits are that a computer algorithm should eliminate any personal prejudices that a judge may hold, and it should be fair to all convicted offenders. The algorithm should improve on the accuracy of human decision makers by taking many more factors into account.
    However, the algorithms work in such a way that it is almost impossible to figure out how they reach a decision, so it is very difficult to challenge the sentence. The algorithms are typically written by private companies rather than government agencies. Whilst the programs can take away the possibility that a judge will be biased against people, the algorithms may themselves be programmed to have biases against particular characteristics.
    There are ethical concerns that the sentencing algorithm used may be biased and that the lack of transparency in how the decision is reached leads to unfair sentencing. [6]
    This question should be marked against the band descriptions and levels of response guidance for extended response questions on page 94.

3. (a) Use of email only for work purposes so that employees do not spend their time on personal email. Users must not download malware so that the computers are less likely to become infected. Users may not eat food or drink near a computer so that there is no risk of spillages damaging equipment. Users must not access social media for personal purposes so that time is not wasted. Use of removable storage devices is not allowed so that malware is not accidentally introduced. Users must use a strong password of at least eight characters including special characters and change it often to reduce the threat of shouldering or guesswork. Users may not use anybody else's computer log in to prevent issues with inappropriate access levels and data security. Allow any other suitable behaviours with explanation. [4]
    (b) To find out who has logged onto systems at what dates and times to see whether an employee was at work or not. To view web logs to see which websites an employee visited which can be used to see if they actively were on websites in breach of the AUP. To monitor staff entry/exit from the building so they know who is on the premises in the event of a fire. [4]
    (c) Social engineering is the dishonest manipulation of people to cause them to divulge data or information against their (or their company's) better judgement. [2]
    (d) (i) Customers may have their data stolen which can be used to steal their identity. This may impact the access they have to their bank account and could result in unauthorised withdrawals. [1]
         (ii) Staff may require further training on how to handle and identify such attacks. They may cause a liability for the bank to repay any money that has been fraudulently withdrawn. They may be formally cautioned with regard to their job. [1]

4. (a) The copyright to the code will be owned by the programmer or company. If they have allowed it to be copied then the team can legally do this. They may have created other restrictions, such as the need to acknowledge the original programmer or release the new adaptation and source code for free. If the team doesn't act within the terms of the licence then they would be breaking the Copyright, Designs and Patents Act. It would be ethical to develop using someone else's code if within the terms of the licence. If outside the terms, it would be unethical as it deprives the original creator of their work and possibly income. [4]

(b) Proprietary: Users have no access to the source code so cannot modify the program.

Open source: Users do have access to the source code and can modify it. They will usually need to provide details of their changes to others who want the source code. [4]

(c) Open source software is likely to be used by more people. This can help boost the programmer's or website's reputation and could help generate income through support services or advertising. Having more users means a greater pool of contributors which can result in faster development of the software. [2]

5. (a) Computer Misuse Act 1990. [1]

(b) Data Protection Act 2018. [1]

Topic 6

The completed Python program solutions to all practical examination question in Topic 6 are available in the folder *Python Exam Practice Finished Solutions* of the download available from **www.clearrevise.com**.

BAND DESCRIPTIONS AND LEVELS OF RESPONSE GUIDANCE FOR EXTENDED RESPONSE QUESTIONS

Level	Description	Mark range
3	• Thoughts, explanations, descriptions and ideas are consistent throughout the response • Clear explanations or descriptions • Evidence and examples are given to support explanations and descriptions • Logically structured response • Both advantages and disadvantages considered if required • Points and examples included that are relevant to the question • Points discussed / explained • At least three points typically required	6–8 marks
2	• Logically structured response • Clear and accurate explanations or descriptions • Both advantages and disadvantages considered if required • At least two points typically required	3–5 marks
1	• A description of some points has been given • Advantages or disadvantages briefly considered if required • At least one point typically required	1–2 marks
0	No answer has been given or the answer given is not worth any marks	0 marks

The above descriptors have been written in simple language to give an indication of the expectations of each mark band. See the Pearson Edexcel website at **https://qualifications.pearson.com** for the official mark schemes used.

INDEX

E

Ebbinghaus iii
elif clause 71
embedded system 34
encryption 63
energy consumption 53
environmental issues 53
errors 7
  overflow 21
Ethernet 46
ethical hacking 50
e-waste 53
execution error 73
external pen testing 50

F

facial recognition 51
fetch-execute cycle 32, 33
file
  management 38
  repair software 39
  size 27
  text file 80
firewall 51
float 67
flowchart 3, 6
  symbols 3
For loop 72, 75
freeware 58
frequency 28
FTP 46
functions 86

G

gibibyte 18
global variable 86, 87
grey hat hackers 50

H

hacking 50, 61
hard disk drive (HDD) 36
healthcare 56
Hertz 28, 33
hexadecimal 23
  to binary 23
  uses of 24
high-level language 41
HTTP / HTTPS 46

I

identifiers 69
if...elif...else 71
images 26
IMAP 46
indexing
  arrays 75
  strings 78
input 68
integer 67
intellectual property 57
interference 44
internal pen testing 50
Internet 43, 45
Internet layer 47
interpreter 41
interval 28
IP address 45, 47
iteration 70, 72
  condition controlled 73
  nested 72

J

John von Neumann 32

K

keylogger 59
kibibyte 18

L

LAN 43
land 36
languages 41
latency 44
layer 47
least significant bit 19
legislation 54
length check 82
licencing 54, 57, 58
linear search 8, 13
link layer 47
lists 8, 75, 76
  searching 8
  sorting 10
local variables 86
logical shift 22
logic error 7
logic gates 14

loop
  condition controlled 73
  count-controlled 72
lossless compression 29
lossy compression 29
low-level language 41

M

MAC address 47, 49
machine learning 55
macro scripts 59
magnetic storage devices 35
main memory 34
malicious code 59
malware 59
man-in-the-middle attack 61
manufacture 53
MAR 33
MDR 33
mebibyte 18
memory 34
  location 67
merge sort 12
mesh network 48
methods 77
  string 78
mining 53
modules 2
most significant bit 19
multi-tasking 38

N

negation 14
nerge sort 11
nested iteration 72
nested selection 4, 71
network 43
  protection 51
  protocol 46
  security 50
  speeds 45
  topology 48
NIC (Network Interface Card) 46
non-volatile 34
NOT gate 14

O

open source software 58
operating systems 38
operators 5, 70, 85
optical drive 36
optical storage devices 35
OR gate 14
output 68
overflow 21, 22

P

packets 45, 47
parameter 87
patch 40, 60
patents 57
pattern check 82
PC 33
penetration testing 50
peripheral management 38
pharming 61
phishing 60
physical security 51
PIN 60
pit 36
pixel 26
pixels per inch (PPI) 27
plaintext 63
POP3 (Post Office Protocol) 46
portability 35
presence check 82
privacy 54
procedures 86, 87
process management 38
programming languages 41
proprietary software 58
protecting digital systems 61
protocol 46
protocol layers 47
pseudocode 4
Python 66

R

RAM 34
range 44
range check 82
ransomware 59
real 67
record 75, 80, 81
recovery 62
registers 33

relational operators 70
resolution 27
robotics 56
robust software design 40
ROM (Read Only Memory) 34
routers 45
routing table 45
runtime error 7

S

sample rate 28
sample resolution 28
scope 86
searching
    binary search 8
    linear search 8
secondary storage 35
security 50
selection 70, 71
self-driving vehicles 56
sequence 70
shifts 22
    overflow 22
shouldering 60
signed integers 20
SMTP 46
social engineering 60
software licences 54, 58
software patch 60
solid state storage 35, 36
sorting 10
    bubble 10
    comparison of algorithms 12
    merge sort 11
sound 28
speed 35
star network 48
stored program computer 32
string 67
    concatenation 78
    conversion 68
    functions 78
    manipulation 78
    methods 78
subprograms 2, 86
substrings 78
switch 49
switches 18
syntax errors 7
systems architecture 32
system software 38

T

TCP/IP 47
tebibyte 18
terminator 48
text files 80
time slice 38
topologies 48
trace table 6
trademarks 57
translators 41
transmission control protocol 47
transmission speed 44, 45
transport layer 47
Trojan 59
truth tables 14
two-dimensional arrays 76
two's complement 20

U

unsigned integers 19
USB flash drive 35
user management 38
utility software 39

V

validation 40, 82
variable 67, 86
    scope 86
verification 40
virus 59
volatile 34
von Neumann architecture 32
vulnerabilities 40, 60

W

WAN 43
Waste Electrical and Equipment
    Regulations (WEEE) 53
While loop 73
white-box pen testing 50
white hat hackers 50
Wi-Fi 46
wired connectivity 44
wireless connectivity 44
World Wide Web 45
worm 59
writing to a file 81

EXAMINATION TIPS

With your examination practice, apply a boundary approximation using the following table. This table is calculated using a rounded average of past years' boundaries for the 1CP1 GCSE course.

Be aware that boundaries can vary annually.

Grade	9	8	7	6	5	4	3	2	1
Boundary	70%	60%	52%	45%	38%	31%	23%	15%	8%

1. Read each question carefully. Some students give answers to questions they think are appearing rather than the actual question. Avoid simply rewriting a question in your answers or repeating examples that are already given in the question.

2. Understand the requirements of command words at the back of the specification. If 'describe' or 'explain' questions are given you need to expand your answers. To help you justify your responses, aim to include connective words such as BECAUSE... or SO... in every answer **because** this forces you to justify your point, **so** you get additional marks. See how well it works! Explain questions such as 'explain why this is the most appropriate...' do not require just a list of benefits. Instead you should identify the benefits and then expand each one, applying them to the scenario or context.

3. Full answers should be given to questions – not just key words.

4. Make your answers match the context of the question.

5. Avoid repetition of responses where more than one response is required.

6. Use technical language and keywords rather than informal language such as 'things' or 'stuff'.

7. Algorithm questions require an actual algorithm not a repetition of the question. If a question explicitly asks for an algorithm to be written in pseudocode, then it will not gain marks if it is written as a flowchart. Equally, a question that asks for an algorithm to be written as a flowchart will not gain marks if answered with pseudocode.

8. If you have difficulties with algorithm questions, remember that you will gain marks (where appropriate) for input and output statements.

9. Generic answers are not sufficient. For example, if a question asks for a description of the function of a router, an answer 'it connects devices together' is not sufficient. Instead answers should describe how routers are used to receive packets from computers, read the destination address of each and then forward each packet to its destination. *Faster*, *bigger* and *cheaper* are not very useful responses unless you justify your point.

10. Arrays will always start at zero. Not one.

11. Remember that a nested loop completes fully for each iteration of the outer loop.

12. Be careful with quotes around strings. For example `choice = A` (which assigns a variable) is very different to `choice = "A"` (which assigns a value).

13. Remember when working out calculations that orders of precedence (BIDMAS) apply.

14. Write clearly and draw neatly. If the examiner can't read or understand what you have written you will get no marks

Good luck!